THE CHRISTIAN WAY OF DEATH

A Zondervan "Reflections" Book

THE CHRISTIAN WAY OF DEATH

by Gladys Hunt

ZONDERVAN PUBLISHING HOUSE
Grand Rapids, Michigan

THE CHRISTIAN WAY OF DEATH

© 1971 by Gladys M. Hunt

Library of Congress Catalog Card Number 77-133362

Printed in the United States of America

Seek God
who turns the shadow of death
into the morning.

Amos, the prophet

Contents

Preface   ix

1. DEATH   15

2. REALITY   31

3. TRIUMPH   43

4. DELIVERANCE   55

5. GRIEF   63

6. SYMPATHY   71

7. CHILDREN   79

8. FUNERALS   91

9. GOD   109

Preface

Today we buried the girl who had been my college roommate.

Yesterday I received a call from her mother, and spoke with surprised pleasure — almost too gaily — until I realized that something had happened.

She said, "We've come back from California to bury our Kathryn in Michigan. Paul and their children are here with me." I hadn't heard of her death till then.

Kathryn was dead. She shouldn't have died now. She was too young. Her children needed her; her husband loved her. Nevertheless, Kathryn was dead.

It was as if I'd died. We'd known we would die when we were older, but not now. We hadn't thought much about death, for life was good and sweet and fun, and now suddenly we weren't the invincible ones. We, the golden girls, the life of the party, the idealistic world-changers . . . it couldn't happen to us. But one of us had died. Suddenly I felt vulnerable.

I thought back over our college years and the silly things we'd done. We had been roommates three out of our four years at Michigan State, both of us journalism majors. We took a year of Shakespeare together from a funny little professor who sat cross-legged on his desk, dramatizing each character until the play lived in our memories. We went for walks and talked about life.

Ours was the party room in the corridor because our mothers sent the best "care" packages.

One Halloween we dressed up and attached ourselves to a group of trick-or-treaters, and later sat on the curb in front of our dorm eating the goodies we'd collected. We went camping, visited each other's families, and laughed a good deal. I still have the telegram she sent when she heard of my engagement.

She was my bridesmaid; I was hers. We rejoiced with each other.

But I have more memories than this. We'd often talked together about God and how you could know Him. We read the Bible together. One day she came into our room, all glowy and radiant the way a Swedish girl can be, and said, "I've met Him." And since men are often the topic of dorm conversation, I asked without much enthusiasm, "Which man is it?"

She said, "The One who lives upstairs!"

Not too orthodox a way of announcing that she had become a Christian.

The last time I visited her in her own home with her own family (a husband and three children who were awesomely like their happy parents), the Bible I had given her at the time she asked Christ to take over her life was on the nightstand by her bed. I opened it and read what I had written on the flyleaf, and all the emotion of our becoming sisters in Christ came back to me.

And so I stood by Kathryn's grave today and wept. She had so much to live for, I thought, though more to die for. My tears were partly out of wonder — that God would put me in a certain hall in a certain dorm so I could be Kathryn's roommate, and she could hear about God's Son and become one of His. I was profoundly grateful.

I wept for her mother because Kathryn was her only daughter. I wept for her children who needed her. I wept for her husband. I wept for me.

Life suddenly seemed so short.

(From my journal, 1966)

1

Death

*Death be not proud, though some have called thee
Mighty and dreadful, for thou art not so.*

John Donne in
Hymn to God My God

Man makes a poor god. He is never more sure of this than when he dies. Worshiping at his own shrine may be a palatable experience in life; it will not suffice for death. Death strips a man naked of his sufficiency. It is the unknown, the impenetrable. A man feels uncomfortable, vulnerable, in the face of so awesome an enemy — an enemy who shows no partiality for age, wealth, or position.

Poets and philosophers investigate death's mystery with imaginations of its misty fog, its darkness, its inevitability. High school students, studying poetry units, still complain, "Why are poets always writing about death?" Death, life's great fact, compels our inquiry. I still remember an English class assignment, involving the last stanza of William Cullen Bryant's *Thanatopsis.*

So live, that when thy summons comes to join
The innumerable caravan which moves
To that mysterious realm, where each shall take

15

His chamber in the silent halls of death,
Thou go not, like the quarry-slave at night,
Scourged to his dungeon, but, sustained and soothed
By an unfaltering trust, approach thy grave,
Like one that wraps the drapery of his couch
About him, and lies down to pleasant dreams.

I memorized it, as directed, appreciated its imagery, but got few comfortable ninth-grade feelings about dying from it, only a sense of majestic departure. I *do* remember special vocal emphasis when reciting "sustained and soothed by an unfaltering trust. . . ." That seemed the most hopeful part of the poem. I didn't like the lifeless sound of "chambers in the silent halls of death." And I was aware that some violent exits from this life betrayed little dignity. Did the poet really *know* about death?

Shakespeare comments in *Julius Caesar,*

It seems to me most strange that men should fear;
Seeing that death, a necessary end,
Will come when it will come.

Francis Bacon wrote that "men fear death as children fear to go in the dark; and as that natural fear in children is increased with tales, so is the other."

They have said the phrases that have become part of our vernacular. *As cruel as death, as hungry as the grave. As sure as death. Death, that grim foe. What is so intricate, so entangling as death?* Poets speak of death's reality freely; most people do not. It has often occurred to me that, facing this great final adventure, men would prepare for it, knowing its inevitability. But most people don't talk about what scares them. We are more often like the man in Jesus' parable: "I will build bigger barns. . . ."

In a sense, every time death touches our lives it is a reminder of our frailty, of our temporary sojourn in this world. John Donne's words remind us that

Any man's death diminishes me,
Because I am involved in mankind;
And therefore never send to know for
Whom the bell tolls; it tolls for thee.

The toll of the bell is a call to evaluate personal values, to get perspective on our being. It can be the most constructive, enlarging and sobering of all our experiences.

Every day more than 5,000 Americans die. Seventy-five percent of these are "processed out" of crowded institutions, most of these dying without the support of a close circle of loved ones or religious faith. In the western world many people, trusting white-coated gods in laboratories, still look to the messiah of technology for some kind of ultimate deliverance from death. Admitting that death is inevitable comes hard. Psychiatrists are now saying that death is the most important question of our time and that fear of death festers a variety of psychoses.

Increasing numbers of people now attain the biblical three score and ten years. Yet, at the same time, our own technology and poor stewardship of earth's bounty threatens life. The atom bomb potentially nullifies the life-extending benefits of new cures and medicines. Some psychiatrists believe a massive panic over death pervades young and old alike in our culture. Neurosis over death, claims Dr. Rollo May, is a basic cause of man's psychic disorder. Dr. May sees obsessive interest in sex as a subconscious expression of anxiety over death.

> An obsession drains off anxiety from some other area and prevents the person from having to confront something distasteful. What would we have to see if we could cut through our obsession about sex? That we must die. The clamor of sex all about us drowns out the ever-waiting presence of death.

> When I strive to prove my potency in order to cover up and silence my inner fears of impotence, I am engaging in

a pattern as ancient as man himself. Death is the symbol of ultimate impotence and finiteness, and anxiety arising from this inescapable experience calls forth the struggle to make ourselves infinite by way of sex. . . . Repression of death equals obsession with sex. Sex is the easiest way to prove our vitality, to demonstrate we are still "young," attractive and virile, to prove we are not dead yet.[1]

When a man rejects God and His claim to raise the dead, he searches for other ways to prove his immortality, for if he is not immortal his life is without meaning. For instance, 1) he may say, "I believe a man lives on in his children, his family or his tribal group." Or 2) "Man may die, but nature goes on," says another who believes in a kind of salvation-through-nature — an extension of the hope of evolution. 3) The educated humanist insists, "A man lives on in his contribution to the world in art, science, music, literature and so forth. As subsequent generations are influenced through his deeds, he is immortal."

For years people have claimed one of these three modes of immortality, asserting their autonomy from God. Recently these theories have left their adherents uneasy. One well-placed bomb eliminates every one of their hopes. Nature itself is vulnerable and in danger of being destroyed in a diseased environment. The future of humanity on the face of the earth is in question. The ecology crusade is an unacknowledged crusade against death. On Earth Day 1970, a small boy carried a placard in a mass demonstration which read, "I want to live," a touching reminder that the earth might destroy its inhabitants, even as we are destroying the earth. A polluted environment, population explosion, predictions of famine, and the grim specter of nuclear annihilation make mockery of traditional hopes of immortality apart from God.

---

[1]*Love and Will*, Rollo May, Norton.

Man, seeking immortality through his own formulas, finds himself backed up to a wall of despair. Nihilism, the next logical step, is a scary concept. For the young person the drug scene offers a fresh attempt to transcend life and its boundaries. How else can one return to the Garden of Eden, a garden without a serpent, a garden where life doesn't push a person, where he is free to "do his own thing"?

Steve, a junior at a midwestern university, recently recounted his own quest,

> I'd look at the stars on a dark night; I'd see beauty around me in the new life of budding trees. I knew existence must have meaning, some design. But I couldn't find out what it was all about. No one seemed to know the goal of life, the meaning of being. I took a philosophy course, and that was a real disaster. The more I looked for someone who knew the answer to life, the more hopeless life looked. I couldn't find anyone who knew the way.
>
> Then one of my friends said that if I'd take some acid (LSD) it would open up new horizons for me. It would show me life as it was meant to be. He was convincing. Against my better judgment, but in desperation, I took a trip and it was a bad scene. I was terrified. The world was distorted; I was grotesque. I was afraid — afraid of life and afraid of death.

Contemporary drama, art and literature scream out this same message of despair. Even the rock sound is a noisy inquiry into the meaninglessness of existence. *Newsweek* magazine, in reviewing six plays by four playwrights, had this to say:

> . . . The thing common to all of them (is) an attitude, a stance, a pulse, a rhythm, a sound, a feel. Perhaps a mathematician could find an equation to express it, say $E=MC^2$ where E= End, M= Modern and C= Civilization. In their various ways the writers are telling us, "Mac, it's all over . . . squared."[2]

---

[2]*Newsweek,* April 28, 1969. Theater section.

Somerset Maugham, commenting on Bertrand Russell's philosophy, writes,

> It may be that, as he (Russell) says, philosophy doesn't offer or attempt to offer a solution of the problems of human destiny; it may be that it mustn't hope to find an answer to the practical problems of life; for philosophers have other fish to fry. But who then will tell us whether there is any sense in living, and whether human existence is anything but a tragic — no, tragic is too noble a word — whether human existence is anything but a grotesque mischance?[3]

If life is incoherent, what of death? If death is insignificant, what of life? Human value hangs in the balance. This phenomenon of mental anguish over death in the young is unique to modern history. Despair is the mood of the age; much of the campus disorder springs from this root. A mystical yearning for the supernatural, for release from the rat race of life — for hope — plagues thoughtful collegians. Men have an insatiable thirst for answers to ultimate questions. The human spirit is not sustained or explained by scientific analysis.

Out of the failure of scientific rationalism to speak to man's ultimate need has surged a stream of superstition. Man, suffering from the disease of extremes, leaves the shrine of scientific inquiry and commits intellectual suicide at a witch's cauldron. Across the country, and indeed in the whole of the western world, people are looking in increasing numbers to the occult, to tarot cards, to black magic for supernatural wisdom. Pollsters and fortune tellers, witchcraft and horoscopes offer the same kind of hope for a message from "outside" that a primitive people expect from a witchdoctor who reads the entrails of a chicken. When a

---

[3]W. Somerset Maugham, *A Writer's Notebook.*

personal God, who has revealed Himself to men, is neglected, what other hope do men have?

Clergymen who have sold out to the once popular god of rational thought have lost their bearings as well. Casting doubt on the biblical concept of life after death, they have no answer to offer their parishioners who face death. Questions about death are curiously sidestepped; society's moral issues are discussed instead. When will someone shout out that moralizing sermons are no substitute for theological hope?

It was the message of the resurrection of Jesus Christ that rocked the first-century world. The claim of the early church was not that it had a superior morality, but that Jesus Christ had been crucified and had risen from the dead. Disciples risked their lives to proclaim the validity of His resurrection and the hope offered to all His followers, "Because I live, you shall live also." They had seen Him die; they saw Him alive again, and that encounter gave them courage to preach about eternal life in the face of death.

> Belief in the resurrection of Jesus is the motive power of all Christian mankind. From what did this faith spring? From five or six remarkably vivid hallucinations? To think so is just as absurd as to suppose that five or six sparks would make water boil in a huge caldron.[4]

This book explores the hope of those early disciples (and, in fact, of all believers back through the Old Testament) that God has prepared for us an eternal glory which goes beyond our short-lived days on earth. Life has meaning and purpose now. The proof of this is that mortality will one day be swallowed up in immortality. Look where you will; there is no hope, no answer like this one. It allows us

---

[4]Dimitrii S. Merezhkovsky in *Jesus Manifest.*

freedom to live and freedom to look at death while we are still living and know a peace which is beyond understanding.

What was your first encounter with death? Can you think back to the time when you first *realized death?* I remember playing "catch the ball" in front of our home one day with our almost three-year-old son. A squirrel ran in the path of a car and then it lay lifeless in the street. One minute a running squirrel, the next a still body that could no longer run. *What happened, Mommy?* Death. A dog. A favorite kitten. And then a favorite person.

The way in which these first encounters fit together probably determines your present attitude toward death. Especially if someone vital in your life was involved, someone who left a huge gaping hole of sorrow. An emptiness that only disappeared when your life and mind was filled with other things. Death *is* hard; it is ugly. Who can explain away its awful tragedy in our lives?

I would not presume to explain *away* death, to write about it in such a way as to destroy its power. I cannot even explain *death;* no human can do that. The best we can do is to see death in perspective by looking at the realities of life in such a way that we see before and beyond this life. Perspective on death is bound up in the character and power of God. We can explain away some of life's mysteries and inequalities, but when it comes to having a perspective on death, I only know one place to turn: to God.

Death can be darkness. It can also be a "covered way which opens into light." That's why the Apostle Paul could write so convincingly, "We do not sorrow as if we had no hope,"[5] and then tells us that what we see now is only "through a glass darkly." There's more to come.

---

[5] I Thessalonians 4:13.

My early experiences with death did not take away its finality or its sorrow. I have never personally felt completely fearless in death's face. But I am grateful to God for letting me know people who received His grace when they needed it. My first close tie broken by death was with an aunt. I was sixteen. She had three children, one only a year old. She had a lot to live for — and she kept on living long after the doctors thought she would die. Her conflict was the human dilemma. She had a vital, personal faith in God and a strong confidence in His ability to do what was best, but thoughts of her family made life seem dear. Like the apostle, she was hard-pressed between two desires. Sometimes she prayed in her pain that she would die; then her dogged determination to live took over and she kept on living.

My grandmother lived next door, and to isolate the family from the suffering involved, my aunt was being cared for by a nurse and my mother in grandmother's home. My cousins were too young to understand all that was happening, and even I, at sixteen, was awed by the solemnity of her pain, by her lack of recovery. A pall of deep concern had seeped into our household.

When I arrived home from school in the afternoons sometimes my mother would ask me to go over to read to my aunt. Most frequently I read from well-marked Bible passages my aunt requested, and the words I read never failed to calm her restless pain. Words from hymns I had known all my life took on new meaning as I read them aloud to her — hymns about faith and heaven. I sat there often, after she had faded into sleep, and read what she had written in the margins of her Bible and wondered about life, about death, about heaven, about God — and about my uncle and their children. Death seemed so unreal, so scary; life seemed so sweet, so necessary.

Something happened the night she died. My mother was

with her, and God did a wonderful thing for my aunt. He showed her something beyond this life. Was it a vision, a dream? She seemed rational and aware. She tried to tell my mother about it; she strained for words to describe her joy. Afterward she was content to leave this world.

I know you hear stories like this. Sentimental stories about death are common (often genuine and enlightening); but I have no intention of making this book a collection of these. I was sixteen, and when I awakened that day my mother told me about my aunt's experience and then added, "She went home early this morning." *Home* has always been a lovely word to me. It's a safe place. Home is the place you belong — really belong. My aunt was earthbound. God graciously opened a wider window for her. She went home. We all sensed this, and it gave a sixteen-year-old girl new insight into death.

Was she delirious? Would she have died anyway that night? Did she see something real or did her psychological need play a cruel trick on her? However you might want to explain this, whether in belief or unbelief, it was real enough to give release and joy and peace in dying. My mother felt herself groping to see beyond; it was that real to her. With all its finality — the awful loneliness of my uncle, the stunned confusion of my cousins and all the sorrow of the rest of us — we were taken beyond the event into eternity's corridors and we saw *home*.

We need this perspective desperately. Otherwise we face life's ultimate without preparation. The only solace for some is to pretend. To think about something else. To play a beautiful piece of music. To over-eulogize. It can be a way to hide. Have you ever been at a gathering where everyone is bent on keeping a new widow from realizing that her husband is dead? Talk about anything, but keep talking because death is too awful to face. Or known the retreating silence of those who are scared of you because you've lost a child? Not a comfortable silence, a frightened one.

That's living life on a flat plane, based on what can be seen. But hope lies in what cannot be seen here. Life is not merely physical; it is also spiritual. In a final sense man's treasures are not what can be seen and handled. What can be seen is passing away. Everything earthly perishes. Only the spiritual is eternal. We know this, and yet we spend ourselves on the material. We often cling to relationships and to our possessions for security. A terrible bondage enslaves us in fear when all our well-being, all our hope, is bound up in a fading existence. To misquote Patrick Henry, "Is life so dear . . . as to be purchased at the chains of such slavery . . . ?"

Abbott speaks of this lack of perspective in his classical mathematical treatise called *Flatland,* in which he describes a world of only two dimensions, like the surface of a table. The people in this world may be straight lines, triangles, squares, pentagons, hexagons, what have you. A person's status and intellectual complexity is demonstrated by having many sides, the most perfect being a circle. Yet seeing any of these approach, others in Flatland observe only a straight line. The story proceeds to build the elements of this kind of society. Suddenly Flatland's security is threatened and unsettled. A Presence comes and demonstrates a third dimension, *space.* Inhabitants of Flatland reject and fear this concept, having lived all their lives in two dimensions. But one character *experiences* a third dimensional existence and thus knows the *joy of being.*

Getting a perspective on death is getting the right perspective on life. It is opening one's self up to another dimension: the spiritual. Coming to grips with death means coming to grips with God and life. We are limited by our concepts of time and space; we need an eternal point of view. Your reaction to death will be conditioned by your reaction to God. Those who are afraid of God are most fearful of death. Those who know Him well seem to welcome the opportunity of being with Him. That's the dimension that transforms death — knowing God.

Young people expect older people to die. What hits a teenager is another teenager's death. Everyone has a kind of subconscious list of who will die before *me*. "I expect to die when I'm old, but not now," we say when death takes one of our peers. "Old age" is always older than we are.

The Scripture describes death in old age rather poignantly.

> Abraham breathed his last and died in a good old age, an old man and full of years, and was gathered to his people.
> Genesis 25:8

Those on in years may begin to lay aside responsibility, get a smaller home, give away their treasures, or watch the obituary notices with new interest. I remember the quiet way grandmother sat in her chair, deep in thought with the newspaper across her lap, after reading that one more friend had gone on ahead of her. "The old men know when an old man dies."[6] The call of their peers reminds them their turn will come soon. But even then, death surprises the living; we are seldom prepared to give up those we love.

What is it like to die? What's beyond? These are questions men ask. And not knowing the answer makes death a tragic enigma. Some say nothing lies beyond. Death is the end. Others say that God is love and if we do the best we can He will see that we have a glorious future. In answer to the first, God has said that eternity is part of man's genetic makeup. That's why man feels uneasy declaring the end of existence. In answer to the second, God bids us listen

---

[6]*Old Man*, Ogden Nash.

to what He says and not fabricate our own heavenly concepts. He has told us what we need to know and has demonstrated His reliability by overcoming death.

I've heard the wails of those without hope — the more primitive and honest displays of grief in non-Christian cultures. Their cries haunt my memories. But I've also seen death transformed by the One who walked through death and came to deliver those who through fear of death were subject to life-long bondage. It's that perspective we are seeking.

When I was a young bride I had a dear friend in her seventies. It was a good friendship. Something young in her responded to me and we shared many things together. She had a quality of life that enriched mine, and simply by being herself she influenced me deeply. In time her body ceased functioning properly and she began to fade physically. When her death was imminent, the clergyman standing next to her bed began,

The Lord is my shepherd . . .

My friend opened her eyes, smiled at those dear to her, and, waving a farewell, said firmly,

I shall *not* want.

It was a statement of conviction. And she, too, went home.

Reality

2

Reality

Walk in the light, and thou shalt own
Thy darkness passed away.
Bernard Barton

I have been having an adventure with death.
When the idea of writing this book was first suggested
to me my response was negative. A dreary subject,
death. I'd rather write about love or life, I thought. But it
was too big an idea to be so easily denied. In the weeks
that followed I met death in conversation, in experience
with friends, and in reading, as if some divine conjuncture
was taking place in my life. With fresh awareness I realized
how unique the Christian way of death is!

My outlines grew rapidly into paragraphs and writing
about death has become a large, awesome experience, like
standing on the ridge of the world with God and understanding in new ways the disastrous scene below, the agony
and sorrow of death, the frailty of mankind — and the triumph of God. Who but God could act in our history to take
care of our deepest needs? No wonder one of His names is
Redeemer.

On a recent Sunday afternoon my husband and I wan-
dered across the campus of the University of Michigan to

hear the University Arts Chorale and Symphony Orchestra perform Brahm's *Requiem,* surely one of the most Christian musical commentaries on death ever written. The magnificence of the message and the music pierced our hearts like swords.

> Behold all flesh is as the grass
> and all the goodliness of man
> is as the flower of grass;
> for lo, the grass withereth
> and the flower thereof decayeth.

> Lord, make me to know
> the measure of my days on earth
> to consider my frailty, that I must perish.
> Surely, all my days here are as an handbreadth to
>   Thee . . .
> Now, Lord, oh, what do I wait for?
> My hope is in Thee.

> Here on earth we have no continuing place,
> howbeit we seek one to come.

> Lo, I unfold unto you a mystery;
> we shall not all sleep when He cometh,
> but we shall all be changed,
> in a moment, in the twinkling of an eye,
> at the sound of a trumpet.
> For the trumpet shall sound
> and the dead shall be raised incorruptible,
> and we shall all be changed.
> Then, what of old was written
> the same shall be brought to pass.
> For death shall be swallowed in victory!
> Grave, where is thy triumph?
> Death, where is thy sting?

> Worthy art Thou to be praised,
> Lord of honor and might . . .

> Blessed are the dead
> who die in the Lord . . .

The triumphant echo of *Death shall be swallowed in victory!* swelled up within us as we walked across campus. We left feeling bigger on the inside than when we had come, caught up in the worship of God. His plan pushed us to new dimensions of wonder. Death, where is thy sting?

Yet in the course of life's social contacts many friends have inquired if I am working on a book, and on what subject. When I reply that the subject is death, the response is, "Oh." Few have asked, "What are you saying about death?" Death. That dread word stops people in embarrassed silence. And when I say that it has been a spiritually exhilarating experience, hardly anyone knows how to respond.

Mankind is frightened by the mere word "death" and nowhere more so than in America, observes English essayist J. B. Priestly. Historian Arnold Toynbee writes, "Death is un-American, an affront to the inalienable right to life, liberty and the pursuit of happiness." In *The Heart of Man* Erich Fromm gives a clear example of this avoidance of the reality of death. "Grief is sin," he writes, giving the psychological rationale for the repression of death. He goes on to urge that man keep himself from even thinking about death. I think such an evasion of reality cannot help but be destructive to the personality.

Death, a subject hard to talk about. Death, a devastating experience to face. Death, the inevitable. Death, my entrance into glory. How comfortingly the writer of Hebrews comments that Jesus Christ came to deliver those who were subject to lifelong fear of death.

Fear of death is no poetic allusion. Unreasonable fear grips many people who take their first flight by air, or any other adventure they feel they cannot personally control. The half-hour delay of a husband or daughter in returning home can fill the mind with uncontrollable thoughts of disaster. Fear for one's safety and well-being marks the lives of all men. It has probably meant human survival; it has also meant human enslavement.

I would not be glib about death. The Bible calls it our enemy; we should not be hesitant to do the same. How would you react if tomorrow you found out you had a terminal illness and your days were numbered? Should a doctor tell his patient his illness is terminal? Would you want to know?

Many studies and much discussion have centered on these questions. I have heard a wife say, "He might live several more weeks if we don't tell him. If he knows he will just give up." I have known family members to lie openly to the dying, "No, you are not dying. You are going to be well." Are three extra weeks of life worth such a lie? Has eternity so little reality?

Doctors say that city people are least familiar with death and most apt to say, "Save no expense to keep him alive." The rural person, in closer contact with the cycle of nature, is quicker to accept death as a fact of life. But increasingly in both city and rural areas, death takes place in institutions and our problems about death are due in part to the fact that we rarely see anyone die.

Our American culture has attempted to so disguise death that we can no longer look at it with honesty. Everyone knows intellectually that some day he will die. And most terminally ill people know they are dying without being told. Some marvelous theatrics take place in hospital rooms as each pretends the other doesn't know and in elaborate conversation attempts to deceive the other.

Obviously, the Christian way of death precludes such deceit. It does not mean that a Christian will always embrace the idea of death as an old friend. But he does deserve the dignity of facing reality and finding that his spiritual resources are adequate for the demands of life.

A doctor's prognosis is always subject to the omnipotence of God. A Christian already knows this. A non-Christian needs to be given a chance to learn this — and other great truths about how to put his life right with God. Telling the truth in a sensible, non-alarming way to a patient at the right time is probably the doctor's job, but he will want either the family or the patient to encourage him to do this. Facing death is too serious a matter for game playing. The stakes are too high.

Not only does honesty allow a person to get his relationships and personal matters taken care of, but it allows him the comfort and sympathy of a close relationship with someone who knows. Patients who are dying can feel isolated, avoided, and very lonely if the truth is not out in the open, at least with their closest loved ones.

A University of Chicago psychiatrist, Dr. Elisabeth Rubler-Ross, interviewed four hundred dying patients in the process of doing research which appears in her book *On Death and Dying*. She found that patients welcomed an opportunity to talk honestly about how they felt in the face of death. She also found that a dying patient goes through several emotional stages which are important to understand. Shock and denial are followed by anger, which overlaps with depression. *Why me?* This is followed by a period of setting things right (which she calls bargaining) and finally an acceptance of death. Such human responses undoubtedly affect Christians, as well as those who claim no religious belief. But Dr. Ross says that those with "religious backgrounds" have greater inner resources in handling the problems they face.

Patients who are dying, says Dr. Ross, want to "hear hope." When hope is gone on earth, God, the source of hope, is still there. He offers hope for eternity. When life's realities are out in the open, this hope can be communicated. Death has ultimately been transformed by Jesus Christ.

Those who have been on the edge of death and returned have said that the last sense to leave is that of hearing. In fact, all senses seem to merge into the sense of hearing. They open their eyes and see nothing. Speech is gone. Even touch may go, but hearing is still alive. Some have commented on the conversations which took place in the room where they lay seemingly unconscious or asleep. How unwise the living can be! It is wrong to assume that the sick person is completely out of reach. The pressure on the hand, the reassuring quiet voice can tell the dying person that a loved one is there and cares. How important to use the voice to say words which communicate hope and peace and love.

Recently a weathered woodsman from the north country told me how he had become a Christian only six months earlier. He said when he was young, in his twenties, he had seen his mother die, full of faith, evidencing peace and confidence that God would receive her into heaven. He had never forgotten the witness of her life and realized that her whole life, full of hardships, had been lived in fellowship with God. Now many years later, his father had died — bitter, full of fear, without hope and without God. He was overwhelmed with the contrast and said, "I got myself over to the preacher's house to say I wanted to believe what mother believed because it was good for living and good for dying."

That's why writing about death is proving to be a positive experience, because the Christian way of death is linked up with the Christian way to live. Life and death are a package. The solution for the first is the grand hope for the second.

This doesn't mean that in the Christian way of death people don't suffer, don't sorrow, don't weep. No. Death can be pretty ugly. And sorrow and tears are real. The Christian way of death simply means that there is perspective which takes us beyond the actual event into eternity, and that God is there.

We need to be better informed about death and more comfortable with its reality. We are not in this alone.

In Maria Augusta Trapp's book *Yesterday, Today and Forever*, she tells of being on tour in California. All of the family had gone, except for a daughter, Martina, who stayed at home in Vermont because her baby was due. When the family arrived at their motel in the city where a concert would be given, they found a message, "Call operator 14 in Morrisville, Vt."

It was one of those moments when the heart actually seems to stop and everything around one disappears in darkness, writes Mrs. Trapp. The phone connection was not good, but the message got through that they had taken the baby and it had died. Then just as Martina was beginning to wake up from the anesthesia, all of a sudden her heart stopped. *Martina was dead.* The family was heartbroken.

In the days that followed the other children asked many questions. "Can Martina see us now?" Questions, questions about death.

> All of a sudden each single one of us discovered a great many burning questions within himself. . . . Someone suggested looking into Holy Scriptures for whatever answers we could find. So we divided the different books of the New Testament among us, leaving the whole Old Testament for Father Wasner. Each one was to search his portion for whatever references he could find about life after death.

> When we met again and each one brought what he had found on Life Everlasting in the pages of Holy Scripture, we were perfectly amazed at the amount to be found.[1]

---

[1]*Yesterday, Today and Forever*, Maria Trapp. Doubleday.

No human is an authority on death. The Trapp family looked to revelation for answers because that is what the Bible claims to be — God's revelation to man. And in the Book they found all the answers they needed to know. As I read of the wisdom of this family in seeking answers, instead of speculating, I couldn't help wondering why we are so slow to seek out God's answers to all of life's enigmas.

I have written of seeing death in perspective. Perspective means the faculty of seeing all the relevant data in a meaningful relationship.[2] Life needs perspective if it is to make sense. What we often see around us is a mad scramble into life's adventures with no idea of how adolescence, education, marriage, the begetting of children, getting and gaining, good works and old age fit together to make a significant pattern in life. Usually the puzzle lacks the piece called death because we have such difficulty admitting that death is a reality.

Reality is hard to face sometimes, especially if the puzzle is going together badly. We are kept too busy moving the pieces into place to get the big picture. Yet the great truth is this: the pieces are easier to place when you have the whole picture in mind. Life and death have meaningful relationships. Facing both is reality.

J. R. R. Tolkien, in his great three-volume epic, *The Lord of the Rings*, with his marvelous use of language, gives us a picture of death that stirs the human heart. Aragorn, the noble king, approaches old age and knows that the span of his life-days are drawing to an end. He thus says to his wife Arwen,

> "At last, Lady Evenstar, fairest in this world, and most beloved, my world is fading. Lo! we have gathered, and we have spent, and now the time of payment draws near. . . ."

---

[2]Random House Dictionary.

Arwen, for all her wisdom and lineage, could not forbear to plead with him to stay yet a while. She was not yet weary of her days, and thus she tasted the bitterness of mortality. . . .

Facing this departure, Arwen, who is not of the world of men, has new insights into the meaning of death for those left behind: the loss and the silence. And she says to Aragorn,

"Not till now have I understood the tale of your people and their fall. As wicked fools I scorned them, but I pity them at last. For this indeed . . . is bitter to receive."

"So it seems," Aragorn replied, "But let us not be overthrown at the final test. . . . Behold! we are not bound for ever to the circles of the world, and beyond them is more than memory. Farewell."

Aragorn insists that the time is right for him to go, and adds this beautiful phrase,

"To me has been given, not only (many years), but also the grace to go at my will, and give back the gift."[3]

A good story always has the ring of reality, as this one does. The parting of Aragorn and Arwen admits that there is no comfort for such pain within the circles of the world. The phrases, *we have gathered and we have spent, the bitterness of mortality, the loss and the silence,* strike respondent chords within us. But more beautiful and true are Aragorn's words about "giving back the gift." Life is a gift. Eternal life is twice so. We become accustomed to it, misuse it, and take it for granted. But it is a gift, not our due. And beyond is more than memories.

---

[3]*The Return of the King,* J. R. R. Tolkien, Appendix A.

Triumph

3

Triumph

Above the ruins of our lives strides the One who today advances the claim that He can authoritatively close the gap between God and man, that He can restore the world deranged by pain, unrighteousness and enmity against God, that He is more than a match for the awful majesty of death.

Helmut Thielicke in
The Silence of God

Margaret had died of cancer the previous week. At our regular study meeting the women who had known and loved her were discussing their sorrow. We missed her; we felt diminished by her death. Two of the women in our group had prayed for her healing and were stunned. "Maybe if we had prayed more . . ." they said.

Another woman had difficulty in coping with the fact of Margaret's death, and admitted she had not gone to the funeral because she couldn't face accepting this loss. One lady was glad that Margaret's suffering hadn't been prolonged. Others commented on the reality of her faith in Jesus Christ and how this had helped them. Each commented, over a cup of coffee, lost in personal sadness, and not even sure others were listening to them. Suddenly one woman burst out angrily, "Why didn't God do something?"

The fog of grief cleared for me. I felt "like spring after winter, and sun on the leaves; and like trumpets and harps and all the songs I have ever heard."[1] It was like an anthem of praise in my heart to be able to say, "He *has* done something."

God *has* done something about death. That's what the message of the Bible is all about. God has done something to redeem us from spiritual death and from physical death. It was not that I no longer felt sorrow at losing Margaret from my circle of friends. My missing her didn't change. It was simply that the fog had cleared. How awful if God had done *nothing*. How amazing that He had intervened in personal concern for us. We had, in the mist, been looking at an isolated fact. We needed to look at a grand panorama of truth.

How many times have we shouted out, *Why doesn't God do something?* And in our ignorance, our arrogance, and our frail humanity we have failed to grasp that He has acted in history and in our personal lives. We look only at partial data.

Death is a fact of life because sin is a fact of life. Death came because of sin.[2] Both are the result of man's choice. Spiritual death and physical death. Given a free will, man chose to ignore his Creator and in that decision he cut himself off from free access to God. He experienced spiritual death.

> For although they knew God they did not honor him as God or give thanks to him, but they became futile in their thinking and their senseless minds were darkened.
>
> Romans 1:21

---

[1] *The Return of the King*, J. R. R. Tolkien, p. 230.
[2] Romans 5:12.

Cut off from God by personal choice. This is man —
wretched, needing redemption, needing desperately to be
brought back into the light of the One who in creation had
said, "Let there be light," and there was light.

Sin brought its imbalance, its consequences to the whole
world: thorns and thistles, the sweat of the brow, pain in
childbirth.[3] The whole creation groans in travail, subject
to the bondage of decay.[4]

A pall of death hangs over life. Physical death is only
part of this — a merciful part. Who would want to live
while forever decaying? No, not that way, you say. But
what of the infant or the one cut off in the fullness of youth?
The mother, so necessary for the full nurture of her children?
The father who is provider and lover? Sin is merciless in
its rampage. Its strength is operative in the world. It is not
rational; it is like a flooding stream.

Death and sin are not God's fault. His love wants us to
freely love in return, not respond as robots. And so He gave
us a choice. He continues to let us choose. We have already discussed the torrent that entered the world at the
first choice made. But evil and sadness do not take God by
surprise. He is still sovereign. He is not a passive God who
set the world running, like a giant clock, and then retired
to His quiet chamber. The record of the Bible, and the experience of believing men, validate His personal concern.
God *works* for the good of those who trust Him. He takes
the yarn of our lives — the sadness and the gladness — and
weaves into the warp and woof His own kind of blessing —
a blessing which defies our normal concepts of happiness.
And in His permissive will, He *allows* hard things to happen. In His mercy He *redeems* these hard experiences and
builds strength into the lives of those who are disciplined by
them.

---

[3]Genesis 3:16-19.
[4]Romans 8:21, 22.

Why does God allow death to strike down a father of five? He is not the author of evil. If He does not raise His hand to prevent the attack, then He asks us to look for a larger plan. He is the Creator, and He has evidenced His ability to create from our sorrows a psalm of praise.

But we are digressing. What has God done about death? He has *conquered* it.

He saw us ruined by our fall. We were unable to climb back to Him, and so, when time was ripe, He came to us. That's what the incarnation of Jesus Christ is all about. Who could conquer sin and death? Only God. And so He came in the person of Christ.

How did He come? As a baby. He entered the stream of human history to identify with us. He never spoke of being born. He always spoke of *coming*.

Why did He come? He said that He came to give His life a ransom for many.[5] He said He came to seek and to save those who are lost.[6]

> He became a human being, so that by going through death as a man he might destroy him who had the power of death, that is, the devil; and might also set free those who lived their whole lives in prey to the fear of death.
>
> Hebrews 2:14, 15 (Phillips)

> He (Christ) has appeared once and for all to abolish sin by the sacrifice of Himself. And just as surely as it is appointed for all men to die and after that pass to their judgment, so it is certain that Christ was offered once to bear the sins of many and after that, to those who look for him, he will appear a second time, not this time to deal with sin, but to bring them to full salvation.
>
> Hebrews 9:26-28 (Phillips)

---

[5]Mark 10:45.
[6]Luke 19:10.

"Behold," said John the Baptist, looking at Jesus, "the lamb of God who takes away the sin of the world."[7]

"I came," said Jesus, "that you might have life and that you might have it abundantly."[8]

"God has done what the law, weakened by the flesh, could not do: sending his own Son in the likeness of sinful flesh and for sin, he condemned sin in the flesh."[9]

God came as man to deal with our sin and with the penalty — death. That's why the angels proclaimed "glad tidings of great joy" at the birth of Jesus. Good news. God has acted in history.

But that's not all. The resurrection of Jesus Christ from the dead validates the fact that God in Christ *has* defeated sin and death. "Jesus Christ has abolished death and brought life and immortality to light through the gospel."[10] So wrote Paul just before he faced his own execution. How sweetly relevant this must have been to him.

The resurrection of Jesus Christ is supernatural; it is congruous with His claim to deity. If God is God the resurrection is not a problem. And there is substantial historical evidence for this supernatural happening.[11] The most convincing evidence is found in the lives of His disciples who proclaimed the news abroad that "The Lord has risen indeed." The death of Christ had left them despondent, disillusioned. They had hoped for so much more. But death, that old enemy, had destroyed their hopes. Then their unbelief and sorrow were turned to joy. He was alive. In subsequent days they were prepared to hazard their very

---

[7]John 1:29.
[8]John 10:10.
[9]Romans 8:3.
[10]II Timothy 1:10.
[11]See *The Evidence for the Resurrection,* J. N. D. Anderson, Inter-Varsity Press.

existence to preach that Christ arose from the dead, thus affirming His victory over sin and death.

It is this victory which is the theme of Paul's writing throughout the New Testament.

> But the truth is that Christ has been raised from death, as the guarantee that those who sleep in death will also be raised. For just as death came by means of a man, in the same way the rising from death comes by means of a man. For just as all men die because of their union to Adam, in the same way all will be raised to life because of their union to Christ. But each one in his proper order: Christ, the first of all; then those who belong to Christ, at the time of his coming. Then the end will come; Christ will overcome all spiritual rulers, authorities, and powers, and hand over the Kingdom to God the Father. For Christ must rule until God defeats all enemies and puts them under his feet. The last enemy to be defeated will be death.
> I Corinthians 15:20-26 (TEV)

> For we know that God, who raised the Lord Jesus to life, will also raise us up with Jesus and bring us, together with you, into his presence. All this is for your sake; and as God's grace reaches more and more people, they will offer more prayers of thanksgiving, to the glory of God.

> For this reason we never become discouraged. Even though our physical being is gradually decaying, yet our spiritual being is renewed day after day. And this small and temporary trouble we suffer will bring us a tremendous and eternal glory, much greater than the trouble. For we fix our attention, not on things that are seen, but on things that are unseen. What can be seen lasts only for a time; but what cannot be seen lasts for ever.

> For we know that when this tent we live in — our body here on earth — is torn down, God will have a house in heaven for us to live in, a home he himself made, which will last for ever. And now we sigh, so great is our desire to have our home which is in heaven put on over us; for by being clothed with it we shall not be found without a

body. While we live in this earthly tent we groan with a feeling of oppression; it is not that we want to get rid of our earthly body, but that we want to have the heavenly one put on over us, so that what is mortal will be swallowed up by life. God is the one who has prepared us for this change, and he gave us his Spirit as the guarantee of all that he has for us.   II Corinthians 4:14–5:5 (TEV)

This is death in perspective, death transformed by the resurrection of Jesus Christ as part of God's great plan of redemption.

Death is unnatural. The separation of the spirit of a man from his body — that's death. And it is wrong and sad. I believe that is the reason why Jesus cried at Lazarus' tomb. He knew He was going to raise Lazarus from the dead and restore him to his family for at least a few more years. Yet He stood at the tomb and wept — wept over sin's power to break up families, over the cost of sin, over the corruption of sin. But He also stood there and said, "I am the resurrection and the life. He that believes in me, though he die, yet shall he live, and whoever lives and believes in me shall never die."[12] Though he die (physically), yet shall he live (physically), and whoever lives (spiritually) and believes in me shall never die (spiritually).

God values both body and spirit. When a man dies his spirit goes to be with God. Absent from the body; present with the Lord.[13] Spiritually a believer in Christ has eternal life now by virtue of his personal faith in Christ. Jesus said, "Truly, truly, I say to you, he who hears my word and believes him who sent me, *has* eternal life; he does not come into judgment, but *has passed* from death to life."[14]

Personal faith completes a spiritual transaction. Eternal

---

[12]John 11:25, 26.
[13]II Corinthians 5:8 (KJV).
[14]John 5:24.

life is a present possession for the living. Death strikes. The spirit goes to God; the body awaits a future redemption.

The body is important to God. What a man does with his body matters in God's sight. When I talk with my husband, I suppose it could be said that I am not talking to his body, but with his intellect and with his spirit. Yet I know him dressed in a body — a total person. The awful shock of death is that the body is there, but it is empty of the person who lived there. It's like a house that no longer is a home.

The beauty of the Good News of God's redemption is that it includes our bodies. God has always cared about the *whole* person. He redeems us spiritually so that we can be alive forever in His fellowship. He also redeems our bodies. It is a consistent theme in the Scriptures; the resurrection of the body. For example,

> If the Spirit of him who raised Jesus from the dead dwells in you, he who raised Christ Jesus from the dead will give life to your mortal bodies also. . . .   Romans 8:11

> And God raised the Lord and will also raise us up by his power.   I Corinthians 6:11

For a glorious doxology on the resurrection of the body, read Paul's words in I Corinthians 15:35-58, in which he answers the question, "How can the dead be raised to life? What kind of body will they have?" He compares mortality and immortality with corruptible and incorruptible. He says it is buried a physical body; when raised, it will be a spiritual body.

> Lo! I tell you a mystery. We shall not all sleep, but we shall all be changed, in a moment, in a twinkling of an eye, at the last trumpet. For the trumpet will sound, and the dead will be raised imperishable, and we shall be changed . . . then shall come to pass the saying that is written:
>> "Death is swallowed up in victory.
>> O death, where is thy victory?
>> O grave, where is thy sting?"

What happens to those who are still alive when Christ reappears? They will be given a new body, as well as those whose bodies have decayed, been burned, eaten by sharks — or destroyed in any other way. The perishable must be made imperishable — and death's power is broken. Read I Thessalonians 4:13-18 for further insights into the glory of that triumphant occasion.

Just as Christ appeared after His resurrection with a body not subject to the normal laws of human flesh, so we will be clothed in a resurrected, immortal body throughout eternity.

This is God's plan of redemption, and it is bigger than present organic life. All of it is labelled *grace*. He did it all, and it is not based on our achievements or good works. The proof of God's amazing love is this: that it was *while we were sinners* that Christ died for us.[15] God has done something about mankind's basic problems. What He has done involves:

> the holiness of God
> the sinfulness of man
> the sacrifice of Jesus Christ to redeem us from sin and death
> eternal life for all who believe.

Before the Gospel can be good news to anyone, it is first of all bad news. God says we can't make it on our own, that our moral failures (whether great or small) don't measure up to His standard of righteousness. He says we need redemption. And that's the moment of truth. Some people don't want to be redeemed: "Please, God, I'd rather do it myself." Which is a pretty drastic position to take when death waits at the door.

Redemption is accomplished and is awaiting the final day of completion. Participation in it is a personal matter.

---

[15]Romans 5:8 (Phillips).

Heaven isn't for those who feel ill at ease with God. They wouldn't be happy there. The invitation is open to everyone to believe — to believe in a way that means handing over the reins of your life to a sovereign God.

God has done something about life and something about death. Trusting God is more than having someone to help you "cross over Jordan." It's getting in on the Triumph of the King, and understanding in fresh perspective what life is really all about.

> The strife is o'er, the battle done;
> The victory of life is won;
> The song of Triumph has begun.
> Alleluia!

Deliverance

4

Deliverance

Deliverance belongs to the Lord.
Psalm 3

We had just finished our family Bible reading. That night it was the story of Jesus raising Lazarus from the dead and reuniting him with his sisters. Our six-year-old son was quiet for a minute and then asked, "If Jesus could make Lazarus alive again, how come He let His dear friend John the Baptist stay dead after that wicked woman had him killed?"

On the surface it did seem unfair. One had a cruel death and the other was given life. That's how it looked to our son, and that is how life's situations often look to us. God acted in one case; He did nothing in the other.

We talked about it for a while. What happened to John the Baptist after he died? What happened to Lazarus after he was raised from the dead? Lazarus was such a sensation that later he was almost the victim of a murder plot at the hand of angry religious leaders! And eventually he had to die again. Was John the Baptist deserted by God in the final analysis — or was he strangely delivered? Is deliverance sometimes life and sometimes death?

The subject came up again a year later when we were reading the book of Acts. Herod, in a fury, attacked the early church. Stirring events are covered with an economy of words:

> At about that time king Herod laid violent hands on some of those who belonged to the church. He slew James, the brother of John, with the sword and, noticing that it pleased the Jews, he proceeded also to arrest Peter. That was during the days of the Feast of Unleavened Bread. Arresting him, he put him in prison and charged four squads of soldiers to guard him, intending to bring him out to the people after the Passover.
> So Peter was being kept in prison, but from the church prayer on his behalf was unceasingly made to God.
> On the night before Herod intended to bring him out to the people, Peter was sleeping between two soldiers, bound with double chains, while sentries in front of the door guarded the prison. Suddenly an angel of the Lord stood beside him, and a light shone in the cell; then, touching Peter on the side, he roused him and said, "Get up at once." The chains dropped from his hands . . .
>
> Acts 12:1-7 (Berkeley)

Furthermore, Peter dressed, put on his shoes, wrapped himself in his mantle, and walked out past the guards; the iron gate opening of its own accord.

Peter's deliverance is an exciting story — and it looks like God went to some work to accomplish it. Chains, guards, iron gates of prisons — and even a man to get dressed and out on the street. But James, poor James. He got it. No deliverance. And his escape looked like such a simple thing for God to accomplish. Just have the soldier miss with his sword, trip over a rock, fall off his horse — anything would have seemed simpler than freeing a chained man in prison.

Have you ever felt like that — that maybe God didn't know what He was doing? Good people, such dear little children, an adored wife — these die while the wicked and ordinary go on living. Or maybe you've tried harder to do right than most other people, and *your* child is the one who is killed on the street of your hometown — or in the jungles of war-torn Asia. Your husband is gunned down in senseless violence. What of this? It seems unfair.

Was Peter delivered and not James? James went to be with Jesus Christ, the One whom he had loved and served. He *was* delivered. Delivered from further persecution, delivered from the confusion that followed the persecution. He was delivered in an ultimate sense. Peter's deliverance seems more real to us, but only because we are so earthbound. God delivers His children. It is not our prerogative to tell Him the best way to do it. And this is good, because we often have foggy vision in the matter of deliverance.

Part of our problem is an inadequate comprehension of what heaven is like. Heaven is being with the King of all the universe, the Creator, having fellowship with Him and enjoying *life* without the impediments of sin, weakness and insecurity. We've never known such freedom and have difficulty conceiving of it. Reading the last two chapters of Revelation regularly would freshen our heavenly senses.

God understands our failings in this area. He made us to delight in what He created on earth. There is a holy exultation in life that is pleasing to God. We rejoice in the magnificence of creation; we sing with the psalmist of the mercies of the Lord. Life is sweet. He means it to be even sweeter than it is. The goodness of earth is only a shadow, a foretaste of what is to come.

The neighbor boy who was staying overnight at our home listened to the Bible story we read. Somehow heaven came into the conversation, and he decided he didn't want to go there. I asked why. He said, "Who wants to just sit around all day with a harp?" Not too many people do. I wondered if he thought of heaven as being confined to wearing pajamas or bathrobes forever! We need to begin to wonder at what the Creator might have beyond this life for His own children to enjoy. Given all the marvels of earth, what will heaven be? The Bible speaks of reigning with Christ, of being joint-heirs, of sharing His glory. What an exhilarating future!

C. S. Lewis, in his marvelous allegory, *The Last Battle,* stirs the imagination in his descriptions of Aslan's country, "where everything is more real — as different as a real thing is from a shadow or as wakening life is from a dream."

> The new (country) was a deeper country; every rock and flower and blade of grass looked as if it meant more. I can't describe it any better than that: if you ever get there, you will know what I mean.
>
> It was the Unicorn who summed up what everyone was feeling. He stamped his right fore-hoof on the ground, neighed and then cried:
>
> "I have come home at last! This is my real country! I belong here. This is the land I have been looking for all my life, though I never knew it till now. The reason why we loved the old Narnia is that it sometimes looked a little like this. Come further up, come further in!"
>
> The further up and the further in you go, the bigger everything gets. The inside is larger than the outside . . . and Aslan is there.[1]

"It was like they were beginning Chapter One of the Great Story, which no one on earth has read; which goes on forever; in which each chapter is better than the one before," writes Lewis at the conclusion of the book. We ought to sigh a little when we think of heaven.

The question of God's deliverance comes up most often in the area of severe illness. Sometimes it is not a matter of life or death, but a matter of suffering or deformity. Occasionally one hears a minister or a healer who says, "It is

---

[1]*The Last Battle* by C. S. Lewis (Macmillan Company, New York).

not God's will that any of you enjoy less than perfect health. If you really believe, you can be healed."

We do read of many whom Jesus healed, and of others healed by His disciples. However, there is no record that He healed everyone. Many must have been unable to get to Him. If healing was of prime importance, would not Jesus have compassionately sought these out? And what of Paul, who said that he pleaded with the Lord three times to take away his "thorn in the flesh" and God's answer was, "My grace is sufficient for you, for my power is made perfect in weakness"? Was Paul's faith too weak?

God *does* heal by removing actual physical problems. He is still the Great Physician, yet most of us think more quickly of seeing the M.D. at the medical center than we do of talking things over with Him. But God also heals in ways that we do not ask. He offers His sufficient grace, the beauty of His character caught in the prism of life.

A "terminal illness" presents a more severe trial to faith. And more severe confusion ensues. Is the medic who says "terminal" omniscient? Should we pray for healing? Can we be sure of God's will before we pray, so that we ask in full faith, not having to add "if it be Your will"? Is much prayer the secret, or much faith? Whole books have been written on the subject of faith healing, and you may want to read some of them. It's a sensitive area. Only be aware of one danger. Do not box God up into your concept of deliverance. He will be God, the Deliverer. And He will *deliver* — some into a larger life on earth, others through much pain with joy, and many into the glory of His presence.

Letting God be the Deliverer means trusting His character in a basic way. It means believing He *is* God. It's a lifetime exercise.

I tried to deliver a friend once. That is, I wanted to stand between the awful hurt of death and my friend, as if I could protect her. One of our closest friends was drowned while canoeing at our campsite. He didn't return from his short trip out into the bay. His wife and children were on the way up to join us for the weekend. The waiting was a nightmare. All night long I pleaded with God to deliver Paul, to let him be found on some island or downshore, lost but alive. I objected when my husband contacted his wife to warn her of our fears for his life. The search parties looked long into the night and were actually in more danger than the original canoe trip involved. But day came, and with it the reality of death.

What do you say to one of your dearest friends? How do you tell her that her husband, father of three, is dead? I wanted to soften the truth, to avoid it, to do anything to save the hurt. I have never wanted so much to be bigger than life. My husband finally helped me. He said, "Don't stand between. You can't deliver her; only God can."

She already knew when she arrived that he was drowned. And I watched God deliver a widow in her grief. He filled her mind and her mouth with His truth and His perspective. He gave her grace to see beyond this life, through all her sorrow. It wasn't what I would ever have planned to demonstrate the glory of God. But it was life — cold, hard life — lived out in the reality of the grace of God. He delivered and He kept on delivering. And He will deliver. It hasn't been an easy road; that's not the point. But He was there, and that made all the difference.

Deliverance involves believing that God's will and His love are the same thing.

> When the righteous cry for help, the Lord hears,
>   and delivers them out of all their troubles.
> The Lord is near to the brokenhearted,
>   and saves the crushed in spirit.
>
> I sought the Lord, and he answered me,
>   and delivered me from all my fears.
>   Psalm 34:17, 18, 4

Grief

5
Grief

I know you: solitary griefs
Desolate passions, aching hours!
Lionel Johnson in
The Precept of Silence

G rief is a smothery feeling. *He is dead.* It is a hard
sentence to learn to live with.

"No one ever told me that grief felt so like fear. I
am not afraid, but the sensation is like being afraid. The
same fluttering in the stomach, the same restlessness, the
yawning. I keep on swallowing." So wrote C. S. Lewis after
the death of his wife.

It is like suspense. Like waiting for what isn't going to
happen. A suspension in time. Does what happens next even
matter? It is like loosing a mooring point and being at sea
— way out, where even familiar landmarks blur.

Joy seems a word never heard and yet the hot prick of
an unexpected memory can tumble joy and grief into rivers
of feeling that leave one blubbering like a child. The river
dries up. What follows is a sensation of drowning in a life
that is flat, dull and barren.

Sorrow is a valid emotion. It should not embarrass us,
nor make us feel weak. Grief is like a journey one must take

on a winding mountainside, often seeing the same scenery many times, a road which eventually leads to somewhere we've never been before.

God does not hand out medals to those who do not weep. Weeping is normal; it is abnormal to pretend there is no sorrow. He made us with a capacity to feel. Remember that Jesus wept.

Grief is an immensely personal thing. It is too big to carry alone, yet no one else can really help. Except God. But is He there? Even heaven may seem hard and brassy. Some want to yell out at Him about the injustice of what He has allowed. Others say all the right things — He's in a better place; she is with the Lord; who knows what God has saved him from? But they sound like clanging lies. We want to shout aloud how much he had to live for, about his capacity to live life as it ought to be lived, about the special kind of happiness he knew.

God understands about grief. The Son of Man is called "a man of sorrows and acquainted with grief."[1] If we understand anything at all about the cross we know God understands suffering. Our grief, our confusion, our doubts, our anger are safe with Him. We can tell Him all of these — in sobs or in shouts — and He *will* hear us. We may have to wait to hear and see Him in return. We can't hear when we're screaming and we can't see properly when our eyes are blurred with tears. But He will wait. We determine our capacity to receive from God, but even here He uses time to heal our exhaustion and tenderness to heal our aches until we want Him.

Sorrow can mix up our priorities. We become absorbed with ourselves in a selfish way, although we don't want to be told this. We meet others who sorrow, but we are sure their grief is not the same as ours. It isn't; it is their grief, not

---

[1] Isaiah 53:3.

ours. And who is to say whether it hurts more to lose a wife or a husband, a child or a parent, a brother or a sister? Our own sorrow is always worse.

We think of the one we lost. We think too much and with too much grief, and instead of the person becoming more real in our memory, the loved one becomes more and more a creation of our own mind, not the person he really was. Passionate grief does not link us with the dead, but cuts us off from them.[2] That's the problem with too many visits to the grave, keeping his room as it was, setting her place at the table — or whatever sentimental tricks we use to try to deny change. We only make the loved one seem more dead.

Last in priority, our thoughts turn to God. Ourselves, our loved one, God. That's the imbalance of grief. Life only makes sense when we reverse the order.

When death hits us we are forced to "try the rope." All the things we have said we believed — will they hold now? For some it is a struggle; for others it is easier to place life in God's perspective. Not without tears in either case, not without the journey of grief. But with a Companion on the journey. I am inclined to believe that special resources are made available to us when we need them, but that our capacity to receive from God and others is determined by the integrity of our relationship to God beforehand. A person who has been regularly drinking at the fountain of living water knows where to go when he is parched and dry. Another, used to digging his own well, may struggle to find the path to the Fountain.

People get over the pain of sorrow. Time is a great healer. Both of these facts are blessings. Still grief dies hard for most people and comes bubbling back up through the years. Perhaps it is easier to experience God's comfort to our spiri-

---

[2] *A Grief Observed*, C. S. Lewis, p. 44.

tual nature, but it is harder to comfort the motherhood, the lover, the child in us that has lost its being through death.

For instance, I find it hard to accept emotionally the fact that one day I will lose my father and mother, unless the Lord returns first. Both of them will have a joyful entrance into the presence of God, having loved and trusted Him for many years. My reluctance to let them go does not mean that I begrudge them heaven's comforts. But something about their being here makes family life closer. When they leave I will no longer be anyone's *child,* a privilege I now enjoy even though I am a grown woman. And what of no longer being a *wife,* a *husband,* a *mother* or a *father!* The sorrow is twofold: missing the person and missing the joy of the relationship.

Grief makes us lazy. We don't plan, for there seems less to plan for. That is why widowers alone become careless in how they look, and lonely widows fail to plan proper meals. A bereaved mother may even neglect her other children and husband, seeming to think more of what was lost than what can still be enjoyed. Or we put up a curtain between ourselves and the world. We shut ourselves off, even from people we love most. Grief scares us and makes us feel things we cannot put into words, and so we box ourselves away from those who want to intrude. A father, losing a favorite son, can also effectively lose his wife and other children in this way.

We need desperately at times like these to turn to the Creator, the Prime Mover in life, and let Him move and motivate us. He can tear down barriers we have built up; He can open us up; He can show us a creative way to use our sorrow. He gives us a future. God wants us to say "yes" to life. Sorrow teaches and deepens us in ways that joy does not. Recently a woman who had lost a child remarked that many of her previous acquaintances seemed surprisingly shallow. It was not they who had changed; she had changed. Sorrow is strangely enriching.

The world is full of people who need love and understanding. The wise and creative person looks away from a past which cannot be altered and finds a way to do some of the loving and understanding. The returns are always greater than the investment. No widow need eat alone night after night when there are other widows who are also eating alone. No mother need leave her arms empty, or long for a teenager to eat her chocolate cake — if she wants to reach outside of herself into the lives of others. I remember reading of a widow who, on her deceased husband's birthday, celebrated the day by baking a cake and taking it to a busy mother with small children. A visit to the hospital, loaning a book you've enjoyed, showing hospitality — there are a thousand ways to send out feelers into the mainstream of life.

People who stand still in life, closed up tight against whatever God might offer, never learn how to let anything important happen to them. Time just runs itself out. It takes courage to put first things first, to risk new adventure, to rearrange existence, even if it means burning bridges best left behind. The adventure of life is not finished. In God's plan for us there is always something new, something exciting and wonderful, no matter what our age. The past is always an apprenticeship for a new adventure, a new rhythm. Yes, even in old age when the final adventure will be death itself. The greatest adventure of all is to know God in new dimensions of life.

In my notebook I keep a good reminder given to me by a friend:

> We are apt to forget that our Heavenly Guide and an earthly guide have different purposes. The one studies to give us an uneventful safe journey; God is interested in the qualities we develop on the journey, not the safeness and softness of the trip.

We expect to be guided wide of every danger and He leads us over mountains and into impossible corners through deep waters of trouble and gets us to Heaven all breathless with excitement and exertion; but fitted for royal fellowship and capacitated for more joy unspeakable and full of glory.   *Author Unknown*

If you cannot bear thoughts of adventure with God right now, don't turn aside. If grief is more real to you than God, don't be afraid. Grief is not a short road for many. The way out is found in God, not in helpful suggestions about ways to live life. Hudson Taylor was led to pray a prayer you may want to make your own:

> O Jesus make Thyself to me
> A living bright Reality;
> More real, more intimately nigh
> Than even the sweetest earthly tie.

Sympathy

6

Sympathy

What sorrow was, thou badst her know,
And from her own she learn'd to melt at others' woe.

Thomas Gray in
Hymn to Adversity

Sympathy. How do you express to a person that you really care because death has taken away someone he loves?

One spring day a little boy in our neighborhood died from a rare disease. The news spread from house to house and women wept for the parents and for the loss of a dear two-year-old. Late in the afternoon men and women stood in groups in front of their houses, discussing the event while their own children played around them. Unexpectedly the parents of the dead boy drove into their driveway. No one had seen them since the news of the death. There was a momentary freezing of conversation and activity, and then neighbors grabbed their healthy, beautiful, alive children and disappeared into their houses. Only one couple did the natural thing – ran over to them in love and simply said, "I'm so sorry," and wept a little.

Didn't the others care? Of course they did. But at that moment they felt almost apologetic for having children who were alive and they didn't know what to say. They were scared by what had happened. Scared and too paralyzed to act naturally.

The inability to be natural in the face of another's sorrow is added pain to the bereaved. In this case, the parents felt that they were an embarrassment to their neighbors, on top of all their personal grief.

It comes in other ways. The widow or the widower feels friends avoiding him or else senses their wondering, "Shall we mention it? What shall we say?" Or the married people who seem almost embarrassed about their happy marriage when another's has just been broken by death. At a time when grief is more than enough to cope with, we ought to act confidently and positively so that we do not add to the burden of the bereaved by our own inadequacy.

The other extreme, of course, is the babbler who says too much — who offers all the glib consolations that make a person want to shout out, "If you think it's that easy, you just don't understand." Job's comforters made long speeches about causes and cures for his sorrow. They had done better when they simply came and sat in sympathetic silence.

It can be awkward to be on the receiving end of sympathy. The bereaved needs his friends so much, but sometimes it is hard for him to take in what they are saying. The burden of relating well in this situation should be placed on the one offering sympathy, not on the bereaved. Comforted are those whose friends stay near, but make few demands on the sorrowing. Being a genuine friend in the hour of death is not easy.

What we want most in our sorrow is the comfort of knowing others understand in even a small measure what our loss means to us. They care that we hurt inside, that we feel bewildered and lost. If we need their advice, we'll ask for it.

Otherwise we just want their psychological and spiritual support. It isn't great speeches that comfort; it is feeling another's sympathy in our awful exposure to humanity's frailty. A pressed hand or an embrace, with a lumped-up throat that prohibits effective speech, the sympathy in your eyes, communicates better than a prepared speech. Tears are not outlawed. Your own most natural way to show that you understand and care is the best sympathy you can offer. If you are an emotional person with a compulsion to weep or go morbidly over the details, show your sympathy as constructively as you can, and then leave. If you are a Christian, pray. It's the best help you can offer. But don't agonize over what to say; simply say, "I'm sorry," or "I am so saddened by your loss," or "I'm standing with you, fellow" — or whatever simple expression is naturally your own. You are not there to explain death; you have come to say you care about the living or loved the one who died.

Don't say, "If there is anything I can do, let me know." A grieving person in a state of shock is hardly able to inform you about what needs doing. If you see something to do, do it. Volunteer specific help. Be as unobtrusive as possible during the immediate aftermath of death when life is confusing. Be sensitive to the conversational needs of the bereaved.

Comfort is a wonderful word. Take it apart and notice its Latin derivatives: com (con — L.) means *with;* forte means *strength.* To comfort another is to come with strength. Sympathy can be comfort; but it is not always the same. Sympathy is a valid way to say, "We're brothers. I care that this happened to you." Comfort is the gift only a few will bring the bereaved. And they will bring it out of their personal inner resources.

A person who fears death does not usually bring comfort to the grieved. He can offer the support of one insecure person reaching out in sympathy to another. Do not think lightly of this. But *comfort* comes from those who have coped with the issues of life and death in their own souls and offer to the other the strength they have found.

It is easiest to offer comfort to believers, to those who know how to trust God even in small ways. Something binds people together who both fellowship with God. It's a family affair as you stand before God together, expecting His comfort and deliverance in the hard hours. It is two people coming to a capable God on behalf of one of them.

When death catches a person unprepared for mortality, sympathy is offered, but comfort is strained. The dimension of hope is not there. I feel personal freedom to speak of praying that God will reach into life with His healing touch. Another's unbelief does not condition my belief. I cannot ultimately deliver any sorrowing person; I can entrust him to the God of all comfort. I can expose him to the comfort I have experienced. And I can be a friend.

Sympathy comes by the bushel immediately after death. And it's good that it does. Facing the shock of events alone would be difficult. But three weeks later, six weeks later, and even more, six months later — when the painful awareness of the loss sinks deeply into our beings — we need our friends more than ever. Most of the time all but a few have forgotten our sorrow.

That's the time for creative friendship. Suggest a definite plan: a luncheon, an invitation for golf and supper. A telephone call, especially at twilight or on the weekends may rescue lonely hours. Share your family. A shopping trip, stopping by to offer a ride on a rainy day, an extra ticket for a concert or play are all ways to ease the recovery of someone who has suffered the loss of a loved one. If a person is not used to going places alone, even going to church alone can be a traumatic experience. Sharing your life and resources is what friendship is about, and it is a practical affair. Make the person feel needed and wanted because of who he is.

In coping with grief many people want to shut off areas of their life, storing away emotions never to be used or hurt again.

> The bustle in a house
> The morning after death
> Is solemnest of industries
> Enacted upon earth —
>
> The sweeping up the heart
> And putting love away
> We shall not want to use again
> Until eternity.
>
> *Emily Dickinson*

In a sense, the love we have for a given person will not be used again in the same way. Love is always fresh and new, but it is also inexhaustive. Love is an action, not something that happens to us. In helping our friends through sorrow, we want to help open new doors and fresh joys for them — so that they can feel more, not less.

Anything that will help the grieving person to know God better ministers to his real need. In sharing yourself, if you are a believer, share your faith. You can hardly do otherwise if it means anything at all to you. Friends learn from each other as they share their experiences in trusting God in life's daily emergencies and in listening to new instruction from Him from the Scriptures. Be a catalyst for spiritual growth by the genuineness of your own excitement at knowing God. There's a comfort in getting God's point of view that can come in no other way. Pray that the sorrow of death will be used to bring your friend into a large place spiritually.

Paul wrote to the Corinthian church about God's ability to comfort us in all our afflictions so that we may be able to comfort those who are in any affliction with the comfort we ourselves have experienced.[1] Our own adventures in God's comforts can be offered to our friends. It is authentic; it is real strength. Experiencing God's release, His answers, His healing is to grow. Growing is enriching. If sorrow produces growth, faith, and love, is it not a better harvest than bitterness, disillusionment and a gnarled soul?

In the final analysis, we offer our friendship, and the quality of our *being* influences others. Whether the *comfort* we offer in times of sorrow is genuine balm or not will depend on the quality of our personal lives.

---

[1] II Corinthians 1:4.

Children

7
Children

Little Jesus, wast Thou shy
Once, and just so small as I?
And what did it feel like to be
Out of Heaven, and just like me? . . .
Thou canst not have forgotten all
That it feels like to be small.

Francis Thompson in
Ex Ore Infantium

A child's fresh, uncluttered innocence — and the fact of death. How does one communicate the latter to the former?

At first thought I gulped at the idea of being responsible for this chapter; who is sufficient for these things? Then, pondering the issues involved, I was overwhelmed with all the data, with the experiential evidence I had that God has life and death in His control. I found myself being thankful

— that God knows what it is like to be human; that He knows our scared littleness
— that Jesus Christ experienced our humanity and took care of death
— that the Christian name for God is *Father*
— that God calls us His children

— that He said He treasured child-like faith
— that the Bible contains the straight scoop on life and
death
— that I've seen it work!

Two things every child must know to insure a healthy view of life or death: one, that he is valuable to God. "Jesus loves me this I know," is simply profound. Made in God's image, a child has worth in God's sight. God does not compare us with each other and choose the nicest. Each is made uniquely different and is special to God. The supreme worth of the individual is demonstrated by the cross. Jesus Christ is God's way of saying, I love you enough to die for you, to take care of your sin problem and your fear of death. Every child needs to visit Calvary and have his heart transformed by God's love.

What we are talking about is evidenced in proper self-esteem. The freedom of a *loved* personality. Loved by his parents, who are God's guardians for him, yes. But something bigger: loved and accepted by God just as he is.

The cross also demonstrates God's holiness. This is the second thing a child must understand. Man's rebellion against God, our inbred tendency to sin, was so awful an offense to God's perfection that its penalty was death. He is as just as He is full of love. In the cross His justice and His love meet. He takes the penalty Himself, destroying the effects of both sin and death, for those who trust Him. Everyone needs the freedom of *forgiveness* and restored relationship.

The cross tells us we are valuable to God; the cross also demonstrates that we can never make it in either life or death without Him. From beginning to end, this is the theme of the Bible. God says, I made you; I love you; you turned away from Me and messed up your life; I have done something about it because I love you.

This is the basic background for understanding the complexities of both life *and* death. We don't begin by teaching a child about death. We begin with "Who loves Patti?" And because we are God's representatives in the lives of our children, they begin to learn from us what His love means and what His character is like. Which means that we have to know ourselves; we can't teach what we haven't experienced. And we don't experience what we haven't believed. They must meet *God,* not our ideas about God. That demands revelation. We cannot know Him unless He has chosen to reveal Himself. The Bible is God's revelation of His love and His character. And when it comments on the nature of man, it is a convincing diagnosis.

The obvious conclusion is this: we must read the Bible with our children if we want them to have an adequate view of God and the world. A good Bible story book could be their introduction to God. When they can read themselves, each family member should have access to a modern English translation of the Bible. In the Bible we meet goodness and evil, life and death. We see God, an all-powerful God, act on behalf of people who trust Him. We see Him transforming lives and defeating enemies. We meet Jesus Christ and see His compassion for the sick and sinful. We watch Him stop a funeral procession and restore to life the only son of the widow of Nain. He cares when people are hurt or hungry. We see Him dying — the just for the unjust — yet death having no hold over Him. We greet Easter together with fresh awe. He was dead and He is now alive!

God demonstrates His love and trustworthiness to us. In such a context, the believing heart of children handles death more capably than most adults. Children believe God can and will do what He said He would do. They let Him be God. Adults want to cut Him down to their size to make Him more understandable.

In the middle of a sorrowful situation involving the death

of a close friend, participants in our conversation kept referring to the death as "an accident," implying that somehow it could have been prevented. I, for one, received comfort in that conversation from our seven-year-old son. He gave a biblical perspective to all of us. He said thoughtfully, "I don't think you should call it an accident. It wasn't an *accident*. God had Vince's place all ready for him in heaven and he couldn't *not* go."

Imagine having your place all prepared and being unwilling to go! Where had he gotten that idea? From Jesus' words,

> Let not your hearts be troubled; believe in God, believe also in me. In my Father's house are many rooms; if it were not so, would I have told you that I go to prepare a place for you? And when I go and prepare a place for you, I will come again and will take you to myself, that where I am you may be also.   John 14:1-3

Death scary? Not if it means going to God's house and being with Jesus. No wonder Jesus commented on the faith of little children.

But let's go back a step to an understanding of *death*. I mentioned earlier an experience of seeing a running squirrel suddenly lifeless. That's the beginning of a child's understanding. His attitude toward *deadness* will be conditioned by yours. You will train him.

Tell him only what you know is true. Is there a heaven for animals, for your favorite pet? We don't know. The Bible doesn't say. God made animals, so they must matter very much to Him and we can be assured that He cares. The Bible says He notices when a sparrow falls to the ground.[1] Maybe God *will* have a surprise for us; but what we know for *certain* must be revealed to us by God in the Bible. Don't let "maybe" become a fact in your child's mind.

---

[1]Matthew 10:29.

This is the time to talk about what makes people different than animals. People can think and talk about ideas and know about God. According to a child's age, we can speak of the distinction between body, intellect (which animals have to a degree) and spirit. We aren't just body. We can demonstrate this by looking into a mirror because we are usually surprised that what we see is us. "I don't feel like that person," a child may say. The part of us that will live forever is our spirit, that real part of a person which can't be seen. Our bodies are the houses we live in.

When a person dies, the real part of him goes to live with God (and don't soften the biblical teaching about the necessity of personal faith) and the house he lives in, his body, is empty. It is healthier, in my opinion, to expose a child to death rather than to protect him from it. Particularly if it can be done in an unemotional context. Better, if at all possible, to meet life's great reality before it involves someone whose departure threatens personal security.

We took our third grader to the funeral of a boy our family had known. The family, including the boy, were Christians, and we knew the man who would be conducting the service would make it not a dirge, but a home-going for a boy whose chances for a normal life were slim from the beginning. It was a time to reaffirm, "That's not the real David. The real David has gone to be with God. That's just the house he lived in, and it is empty now." It was not morbid; our son thought David was quite privileged to go to heaven.

Opinions on exposing children to death vary, and some people would have difficulty carrying off a situation like the one above. We traveled abroad shortly after the death of President Kennedy, and whenever we met British friends, eventually the wife got around to asking me about the "frightful" thing Mrs. Kennedy did in taking her children to the President's funeral, permitting young John to salute the casket and all. Each time I explained, without understanding

English custom, that it was not uncommon in America to expose children to the reality of death and that in this particular case, the Kennedy children were taking part in American
history as well as their father's funeral. Later, in England,
the wife of an acquaintance died, and I realized it was
more typical for the British to spirit the children away to a
relative's home and bring them back only after everything
surrounding their mother's death was a matter of history.

While not wanting to glory in the macabre, I feel that
death is a fact of life to which children must become accustomed. It was just as well not to have our child meet
death for the first time when his beloved grandmother died.
However, this cannot always be arranged. And if death
should come without such preparation, we are still shut up
to the mercy and healing of the same God we have known
in life's other preparations — and it is safe.

Let me return to the point of telling a child only what is
true. Stories about little lost angels who look like children,
and cartoons of the departed, riding clouds and playing
harps — these are a lot of nonsense. We do not become angels when we die. According to the Bible angels are a special kind of creation in God's heaven. They are God's mes-
sengers to serve Him and, according to Hebrews 1:14, in doing God's will they also minister to us.

When believers die they go to the presence of God. Jesus
said to the thief on the cross who believed in Him, "Today
you shall be with me in paradise."[2] The Apostle Paul said
that to be absent from the body meant to be present with
the Lord.[3] When Christ comes again to complete history
and take believers who are still alive out of the world, then
He will give us resurrection bodies (see chapter 3 of this
book) so that our whole person will be redeemed from

---

[2]Luke 23:42, 43.
[3]II Corinthians 5:8.

death, including our bodies. That's why we say the body "sleeps" in death. It will be rejoined to our spirits and remade into a body that will never know the hurts of life. But suppose a child asks, "Did Uncle John go to heaven?" when Uncle John never gave any indication in his lifetime that he cared about God or heaven or even simple morality? Most people want to rush in with an affirmative answer even though they feel uneasy inside. I don't believe the question demands a yes or no answer. In the final analysis, who enters heaven is God's business, and we can never be certain of what has transpired in a person's inner life — or even in the last moment of life. "I don't know" is a good answer for mortals who have inadequate information.

Questions like these provide good opportunities for dialog about what makes *anyone* worthy of heaven. The Bible says that those who have personally trusted Jesus Christ become God's children. These demonstrate their faith by living in a vital relationship with God, trusting Him for the details of life and death. Nowhere in the Bible are we told that God keeps a list of our good and bad deeds and that if the good outweighs the bad then we are heaven-bound. Being a member of God's family is not based on good works, but on personal faith. (Being God's children means we want to do what is right, but this is not to gain the status of *son* and *daughter* anymore than we do what is right to earn sonship in our human family. Doing what is right is the natural product of a love relationship; we want to please God.)

Because death is such a trauma in life we often entertain foggy, sentimental notions about it. Only recently I read of a woman who had an experience of feeling God was with her. She said, "Then I knew that God was also with my husband who died two years ago." That bothered me because it isn't true to biblical facts. Where did she think her husband was in his deceased state that God would be *with* him? Was he with *God?* is a better question. When we give wrong answers to children supposedly to soothe them, we lead them into a mist of unreality.

God's truth is comforting; our fabrication of beautiful stories is not. I remember a grandmother in our town who told her grandson that his deceased father was now a star in the sky. The little boy looked across the vastness of the sky, wondering which was his father, feeling twice as lonely and forlorn as he would have if he had been told the truth.

God has a plan; our children need to know this, just as we do. We don't tell all of this at one time to a very small child anymore than we tell all the facts of other parts of life at one time. We take life's situations as they come and use them to share our own knowledge of God.

A teenager suffers most when death strikes someone he loves. The insecurity of moving from childhood to adulthood, not always understanding one's self, is hard enough. When that security is further threatened by death, life can seem pretty frightening. The greater the individual's commitment to God, the more comfort is available. It is not difficult to see what a source of strength a healthy confidence in the authority of Scripture would be to such a child.

Honesty and openness are essential with teenagers. Grief must be talked about — not in forced conversations — but at sensitive moments. At such a time we need more than ever to say to each other, "I need you and you need me. I feel like you do," and so close the ranks and make life as stable as possible.

"What was my dad like?" Any child who has lost a parent at an early age wonders what relationship she missed, what model for life she never knew. A son wonders if he is like his father or what advice his father might have given him in a perplexing situation. In our struggle to find our own identity we need to know our heritage.

While this "wondering" is plaguing the child, a parent

may be building a new life — not without important memories, but with a determination to live in the present and make life meaningful. The parent knows the past; the child does not. A wise parent takes walks into the past with a child and acquaints him with the people he needs to know. This is true of parents and grandparents in particular. Introducing deceased brothers and sisters needs special sensitivity so that the lost sibling doesn't become a monster rival in a kind of unrealistic goodness and perfection. But we need to know who we belong to!

In counseling university students over the years I am impressed with the importance of parents facing their children's loss with a linguistic solution. *Talk.* Share memories, the small moments which enrich a child's self-understanding. A child recognizes the implications of his loss years after parents have coped with their own sorrow. When parents are a closed box about the past, a teenager's identity crisis seems to heighten.

Only recently a university girl shared with me her personal anxiety about her relationship with boys, her tremendous need to belong to someone and some of her unwise judgments about what made a relationship valid. Discussing her life situation, I discovered that her father had died when she was eight years old. She had been her daddy's little girl. Another father replaced him two years later, but at the age of ten she couldn't make the transfer of relationship, not the same kind of relationship she had before. She was still looking for a place of safety on her daddy's lap! When I said this to her, we proceeded into new areas of understanding herself and her needs. Her mother could have helped her see this a long time ago if she had been aware of her daughter's needs and had been more open to verbalizing the past. Some areas of life are made more secure and decidedly richer by remembering!

It is great to be acquainted with a God who has access to

our children's hearts as well as our own. All of life's answers are found in Him. He is not limited by life's circumstances. He can reach down into a little child's heart or the heart of a silent teenager and provide just the right comfort. He can do that for anyone who will let Him.

Funerals

8

Funerals

We brought nothing into this world, and it is certain we can carry nothing out.

Paul's letter to Timothy

D eath is not beautiful. The undertaker's cleverest handiwork cannot make it so. At death the body becomes an empty tent, the abandoned house where someone once lived — cold, lifeless, mortal. The sting of death is real; it will disappear only when mortality puts on immortality, when the corruptible puts on incorruption.

Death occurs; a loved one is gone; a body remains. In that one sentence are the cold, hard facts of life. The stunning grief, the shock of the loss are enough. Yet a body remains. We cannot fool ourselves. In one sense we know the body is worthless without the spirit, yet it is the physical expression of the person we knew. It, therefore, has dignity and a value identified with our own value. What to do with the body is a problem which has faced man since death began, and the rituals surrounding death, different in each culture, have evolved from this uncomfortable necessity.

And perhaps it is a hidden mercy. If the body were spirited away at the moment of decease death would seem even more unreal. The body is a reminder of a grim reality. Death takes some getting used to, and the details surrounding death's arrangements can be part of learning to live with the facts. An unrecovered body in the event of death often leaves the bereaved at loose ends, as if they wished for a final act to perform.

Funerals are a way to care for the body of deceased ones. But they are also for us. Whatever the ritual we perform, we do it partly to verify the dignity and importance of living in the face of the indignity of death. Most people have thought very little about the history of contemporary practices. Death occurs and the bereaved are swept along into a prevailing custom without realizing what they are doing, why they are doing it, or if they want to do it that way.

Over the centuries, in a variety of cultures, handling the body of the dead has run the gamut from funerary extravagance (the embalming of Egypt) to the quickest possible disposal of the body (Hindu burning ghats and contemporary cremation).

In early America taking care of the dead was a family affair. People died at home. Family members or close friends washed and laid out the body; a local carpenter constructed the coffin; the church sexton had the grave dug; the service was held in the church or in the home. With friends and relatives present, the body was laid in the church graveyard, a meaningful reminder of Christian hope.

In the primitive life of frontier areas, death held even more intimate involvements — unmarked graves in untracked areas, dug by a husband or a son, the simple service spoken by a family member or friend. No camouflage for death here.

Times change. In the 1900's life became "nicer," partly because of the industrialization of our country. Large segments of the population moved to cities; people needed and could afford more help in burying their dead. The role of the modern funeral director is a relatively recent one. Even as late as 1900 embalming was an exception rather than a rule. As affluence increased, the public's expectation of what a funeral director must perform also grew. Fancier hearses for the common man, more elaborate ceremonial touches and, as the details of death moved away from the church and family, the posh funeral home became part of a cultural expectation.

The vast societal changes ushered in by the industrial revolution could not help but affect all areas of life. "Scientific thought" made man feel more capable, more able to control his destiny, and less dependent on God. In Europe the higher critical approach to Scripture swept the continent in the later 1800's. By the early 1900's it had spread to America, casting doubt on the reliability of Scriptural revelation, moving off-center of the message of hope and peace. Glorying in man, the religious establishment focused on man's ability to solve man's problem. Huge segments of the church no longer had a convincing word for either life or death. Ministers trained in liberal theology had less and less to say to their parishioners about dying.

Dying increasingly became an embarrassing concept in a society where few knew the answer to death. People began to look to the funeral director for the help they had once received from the church and the community. And where death cannot be faced, it must be obscured as much as possible. Thus some of our contemporary customs carry an aura of death-denial about them.

When death's reality must be obscured, there are two ways to do it: 1) cosmeticize the body of the deceased, clothe it in finery, give it the best of everything — to glory in the body with a kind of extravagance designed to defy death; or 2) dispose of the body as quickly as possible, avoid the corpse, remove from the scene that hideous reality. Death obscured, repressed or swiftly dismissed reflects the heart of the living relatives, however, not that of the funeral director. The care of the dead will generally bear the quality mark of the lives of the living.

Many a husband, concerned about the present high cost of dying, has remarked to his wife, "When I die, just put me in a pine box and bury me the same day. Forget about all the fancy finery. It's not me anymore; it's just a lump of clay." Or something like that. Maybe it's a suggestion for cremation. Whatever, the emphasis is on the inexpensive and the unpretentious.

Taken superficially that sounds sensible. Especially if a person has witnessed extravagantly emotional displays that were more death-denying than death-affirming. But it isn't that simple on several counts.

"Pine box" equals a simple wooden casket in most people's minds — the simplicity of wood, no adornment, just the sheen of polished wood. Maybe pine doesn't polish up that way anymore, but the "simplest" wooden casket available is second in expense to a bronze casket. Unless you can hire a carpenter to put together a pine box, you'll have to be content with a cloth-covered wooden casket.

Whether it is a burial or a cremation, with today's involved processes of opening a grave, installing a vault (state requirement in some places), getting medical releases, burying a person "the same day" is not as easy as it sounds. Cremation is a quicker removal of the body, but its actual cremation is not always immediate. I mention these details only to point out that we often don't have facts to back up our most earnest statements.

But there are more important considerations than these. What is the Christian view of the body? It is at this point that we need to think through a Christian philosophy for the care of the dead.

Throughout the Bible, the body is seen as good — an instrument for the expression of personality. For fulness of life man needs a body. That seems a facetious statement until we remember that God also says we need a body for the life ahead of us. We will not be disembodied spirits throughout eternity. The Scripture says clearly that our bodies will be raised incorruptible, no longer subject to decay. "The power that raised Jesus Christ will also give life to your mortal bodies" (see Chapter 3). We affirm this great truth each time we say the Apostles Creed, "I believe in the resurrection of the body. . . ."

The Christian view of the body is unique in the world. In Greek thought the body was held to be evil. Plato speaks of the body as an impediment in the search for true being. He reports Socrates in the *Phaedo* as saying that in the life to come we shall get rid of the foolishness of the body and be pure, and hold converse with the pure. Bernard Shaw picks up this heresy in *Man and Superman* and speaks of escaping this tyranny of the flesh, of being a ghost, an appearance, an illusion . . . in a word, bodiless. Eastern religions hold this same low view of the body and of all matter. Confused by the biblical instruction to reject the "works of the flesh," early Christian ascetics fell into this error when they thought this meant they must deny the body. But Christ teaches plainly that evil comes from the heart of a man, from his inner desires. The body is good. What we do, therefore, with our bodies has always been important to God. He refers to a Christian's body as the temple of the Holy Spirit. Our bodies are so important they will be raised from the dead!

It seems fitting then, that at death, the body should be treated with the respect and dignity which reflects the value of personhood. We reject the idea of dumping dead bodies in the street like ordinary rubbish as happened in the sweeping terror of ancient plagues. The dignity of man in life necessitates some comparable dignity in death — not so much for the sake of the dead person, but for those who are still alive and feel the attachment of their personhood to that of the deceased. At death we reaffirm the worth of the total individual.

In the Bible when the patriarch Jacob (called Israel) died, he gave a charge to his sons:

> I am to be gathered to my people; bury me with my fathers in the cave that is in the field of Machpelah, to the east of Mamre, in the land of Canaan, which Abraham bought with the field from Ephron the Hittite to possess as a burying place. There they buried Abraham and Sarah his wife; there they buried Isaac and Rebekah his wife; and there I buried Leah . . .   Genesis 49:29-32

When Jacob died, his sons carried out these specific instructions, a large entourage leaving Egypt to go to the plain of Mamre. Since he died in the land of Egypt, his son Joseph, who was a high official in Egypt's economy, followed the Egyptian practice of embalming in an otherwise Hebrew family funeral.

When it came Joseph's time to die he spoke to his sons, saying, "I am about to die; but God will visit you and bring you up out of this land to the land which he swore to Abraham, to Isaac and to Jacob . . . and you shall carry up my bones from here." Four hundred years later when Moses led the exodus of Israel's children from Egypt's bondage, they remembered and took Joseph's remains with them.

This same respect was shown to the body of Jesus Christ when His disciples took it from the cross, prepared it for burial and laid it in Joseph's tomb. The specific customs of embalming or the use of spices may be cultural; the care for the body of a man is not.

William Gladstone is quoted as saying, "Show me the manner in which a nation or community cares for its dead, and I will measure with mathematical exactness the character of its people, their respect for laws of the land, and their loyalty to high ideals." Although he was neither an anthropologist nor a sociologist, Gladstone's comment simply amplifies that attitudes toward death and practices at the time of death evidence the quality of group life.

Jessica Mitford in her popular criticism of American funerals, *The American Way of Death,* refers to the "full-fledged burlesque of the funeral industry," and when a funeral fits that description, it does reflect the value structure of the people involved. She advocates the low-cost memorial societies which she has helped spawn. Upon investigation, I find that these, too, reflect the value structure of the people who promote them. Each reveals a view of man, an attitude about death and future hope, and though the outward form may vary, the inward substance is often the same. It is our attitude, more than the actual method, which comments on our view of man.

Obviously the treatment given his body does a dead man no good. It is simple folly to believe that a delay in decay by an airtight casket or a vacuum-sealed vault is of any value. Flesh decays. It should and it will. Job faced squarely the fact that worms would destroy his body. A body which returns to the dust is no more a problem to God, when it comes to resurrection, than a body burned in cremation or eaten by sharks or vultures. "All flesh is as grass. . . ."

But I have fresh conviction that the way the living handle death is a statement of their view of the unique value of the deceased, as well as their own value. Death is always more than a biological event or nature's planned obsolescence.

The second consideration necessary to realistically handle the "pine box" theory involves our mental health in facing reality. The anguish of grief is real. Death comes as a terrifying blow. It is not easy to get used to. I would not view lightly the value of a waiting period between death and funeral or memorial services as a valuable time to experience the support of friends and loved ones and get used to the fact of death. In Jewish tradition where the body is buried within a short time, the family and friends gather for a daily proscribed period of mourning. Many psychiatrists support the theory that death rituals are not necessarily cruel exploitations, but necessary grief therapy.

Obviously, circumstances temper our needs. Sometimes there is no body to dispose of at all, and death seems unreal, almost as if those behind are waiting for the event to be completed. In another instance, a lingering illness may have prepared the family for loss, and death comes as a strange mixture of relief and sorrow. Psychological needs vary, and in the shock of grief, we are not always sure what our needs are. Most burial rituals have come into being as an expression of some need the living have to experience group help in coming to terms with the grief they face — a need which has only begun to be met by the rituals.

Grief therapy is no small thing. We cannot simply close off rooms in our heart like closing a door in our house. If a person cannot weep at loss, something is strung up too tightly inside of him. Tears are not weakness; they are God's plan for emotional release. Anxiety is compounded when efforts are made to deny the depth of death's impact. Probably the times of greatest emotional need in human life are during infancy and when death occurs.

Geoffrey Gorer, an English anthropologist, in his book *Death, Grief and Mourning* comments at length about community help in enduring grief. In studying the behavior of those who try to ignore their feelings of grief, he comments, "I had the feeling that, by denying expression of their grief, they had reduced their lives to triviality . . . to meaningless 'busyness' through the private rituals of what I have called mummification to the apathy of despair. . . ."

Surely any public service held at the time of death does not end the time of mourning, but studies done by some psychologists and sociologists seem to confirm that community help in expressing grief is healthy and that a time for public mourning helps a family face the most acute type of deprivation they will encounter.

Viewing the body is the custom most subject to debate. Again, I believe this depends on the needs of the living. A corpse *is* an affirmation of death's reality. But a closed casket affirms the same with quiet dignity and privacy in death. Yet for some viewing the body relieves their personal threat of death. Every one has a feeling for his own body and viewing a dead body may curiously reassure the person about the value, the aliveness of his own body. On the other hand a neurotic refusal to view a body could mean an inability to admit the fact of death and our anxiety about it. In between these are a variety of emotions and personal convictions. The decision must be a family decision based again on personal need and conviction, rather than on public opinion. That is why it is well to think through a personal philosophy ahead of time.

I do not believe one practice is more Christian than another. The attitude which surrounds the custom is of primary importance.

It seems obvious, but it bears repeating — any ritual surrounding death is not for the dead, but for the living. In paying respect to the dead person we are telling the remaining loved ones that we valued the deceased and we care about the living. When the display of the dead body becomes more the focus of sympathy calls than the grieving family, something is amiss in our value structure. (For this reason, if the casket is open, it would help if the viewing room were separate from the place where a visitor meets the living members of the family.) We are not there to glorify a dead body. As my own minister commented, "It is more important to look the widow in the face and share sincere sympathy than to look at the corpse and comment on how natural he looks." Something insecure in us rivets our attention away from the need of the living to focus on the body of the deceased when it is the center of the encounter.

In small towns and rural areas, families do not greet friends in the funeral parlor. Everyone knows where the bereaved family lives and comes to their home to make calls. In urban areas, increasingly friends call on the family at the funeral parlor and do not take time off from work to attend the actual funeral service. Whichever way, it is the sympathy of friends and their physical presence with us that offers the human support we need.

Anyone sensitive to human need knows that viewing the body is not synonymous with offering sympathy and comfort. The strangest of all perversions in funerary practices is, in my opinion, the relatively new idea of the drive-in funeral home. Here the deceased can be viewed in a public display window from the privacy of one's car. Friends may drive up, view the body, leave a calling card and pass on with twentieth-century efficiency. When the pressures of living lead us to support such impersonal, gross practices under the guise of "paying respect to the dead," then we know little of human dignity or compassion. Caring for the body of the dead does not include such marketplace techniques. The wounds of death need some privacy.

I mention these things because we live in a rapidly changing society with human needs which remain relatively constant. Our customs need to be open to scrutiny and re-evaluation, and the fast pace of contemporary life will augment new patterns of behavior. Already the mobility of life has given people a sense of rootlessness and destroyed strong family cohesiveness. Death, without the emotional investment and care of other family members, can be an incredibly lonely experience. When dying is given an increasingly impersonal and unimportant quality, in turn life itself seems more unimportant and impersonal. Some of our present practices may alter simply from lack of group support — a potentially dangerous situation if changes do not take into consideration the psychological and spiritual needs of a person — of what it means to be human and vulnerable.

Our society has both the freedom and need to examine afresh what a Christian funeral should be, but not without great sensitivity to what is already happening sociologically in our country. The recent move against the structural monopoly of the funeral establishment in controlling the ritual of death may be legitimate, but a ritual there *will* be. We need to take care that in disposing of one ritual we do not take up another which minimizes human values.

Robert Fulton in his book, *Death and Identity,* makes a relevant observation about the shift in societal structure.

> The denial of death and deritualization of mourning growing apace in America today parallel and reflect other significant changes apparent in family life. These changes can be identified briefly as: 1) from predominance of the religious to predominance of the secular, 2) from a large group to a small group, 3) from a stable to a mobile group, 4) from an adult-centered to a child-centered family, 5) from a communal family ideology to a democratic one, 6) from an integrated to an individualized group, and 7) from a neighborhood-enclosed family to an isolated family in an urban environment.[1]

The church increasingly needs to be the stabilizer of family life, offering community strength to wavering human need. If the church fulfills its commission it will be pressed into more and more involvement in both matters of life and death. The pressures of life will demand it. And perhaps from the church will come a distinctly Christian way to handle the ceremonies of death in a pagan society which are different from any we know now.

---

[1]Published by John Wiley & Sons, Inc. (New York).

The Christian way of death takes man's needs seriously. The Christian message speaks openly to real people about real things; it is not an escape device. Hence, the Christian way of death should give evidence of the value of the body, the integrity of individuality, the honesty of grief, and the hope beyond the sorrow. Whatever ritual is used, and customs vary within Christianity and within our own country, Christian burial is not a time of denial but of re-affirmation.

A Christian funeral or memorial service is one that expresses Christian hope. The community of the living support the remaining loved ones with concern and sympathy. It affirms the uniqueness of individual personality and the social character of human existence. In a world that is essentially materialistic, a Christian funeral gives a strong statement of faith in that which cannot be seen. It is an acceptance of reality, of deep feelings and a restatement of truths which give meaning to life.

A Christian funeral does not equate the worth of a man with the expense of the casket or the number of floral pieces. Indeed, the Christian view points away from ostentatious display to spiritual reality. The more recent trend to substitute memorial funds for perishable flowers makes sense to the Christian. A Christian funeral is a statement of hope, not a final social event. Some churches drape the casket during the service, minimizing its quality, making all men equal in death. A Christian funeral does more to speak to the question of death than to eulogize the deceased, and uses the Scriptures to offer comfort. How alive biblical truths sound in the face of death!

Some Practical Considerations

Willing one's body for medical research is growing in popularity. If not the whole body, vital organs can be given which offer new hope to the living. A Christian view would support either of these plans, although this is the kind of personal decision which should have the support of the closest loved ones. Plans must be made ahead of time. A certificate bequeathing the body or parts thereof for medical research must be signed in advance, and can be obtained from your lawyer. Research centers vary in their need for bodies and in what contributions they agree to make to transportation costs.

Arrangements ought to be made on other levels of funeral planning as well. Personal wishes should be expressed and written down after some research has been done. Pre-planning forms are available and can be filed with a funeral director, but it is also adequate to have these instructions written down at home if other family members are informed of the location of such papers.

At the time of death those making arrangements are often in poor shape to do so. Sometimes people don't even know a funeral director to call. Most have limited experience in choosing caskets, vaults, and making decisions regarding finances for funeral arrangements. I'd like to see a return to the help of the church in matters of death. Ministers, who are fulfilling a pastoral role, could be informed about services available, about reputable firms and adequate burial plans. I asked funeral directors about ministerial help in making arrangements, and found it to be rare. Yet I do know of the wise counsel other ministers have given widows of meager means in making arrangements. Love and sorrow combined can produce poor judgment in financial responsibility, especially if an element of guilt is present. A man who genuinely does the work of a pastor will not usurp family rights or privacy, and is a more objective source of help. Personally, I would also like to see funeral/memorial services held in the church when adequate facilities are available.

How much do funerals cost? That depends partly on where you live. The national average of overhead costs for funeral directors in 1970 was $726.00, exclusive of the casket. That means in some cities the basic costs will be higher; in low overhead areas the cost will be appreciably less. In a large Detroit, Michigan, funeral home the cheapest funeral, including a cloth-covered wooden casket, is $763.00. Add to this the cost of the grave site, the vault, and opening and closing the grave. In an average Detroit cemetery a single plot costs $200. Opening and closing costs approximate $175.00. If a vault is required these vary in price: a concrete box, $100.00; a sealed concrete box, $135.00; asphalt and plastic lined, $225.00; asphalt, copper-lined, $1000.00.

More expensive caskets can run the cost up considerably. For instance, a solid copper casket runs approximately $2100.00. (When Mrs. Anna Dodge died, the newspaper noted that she was buried in a one-ton bronze casket and that only three of its kind exist in the country.) The subtle pressure to equate elegance of casket and security of vault should be resisted in the Christian way of death. Most reputable funeral directors will not bring such pressure to bear. It costs a good amount to take care of the body of the deceased, even when it is done most simply.

In our university town about ten to fifteen percent of the deaths are handled by cremation, most of these pre-arranged through a funeral director. Costs involve approximately $300.00 for a wooden coffin, plus the crematory fee of $75-100.00. In some states rulings indicate that cremated remains must be buried in a legally established cemetery, which would necessitate purchase of a site. In other places, urns must be purchased with a niche in which to place the urn. Added to this are costs for transporting the body and the filing of papers.

Funeral directors say that between ninety and one hundred-ten man-hours are involved in the average funeral, plus the use of facilities and vehicles. The public has responded to the plusher facilities of the nicer funeral homes, and have thus raised the cost of funerals across the country. Funeral costs obviously would be considerably less were the funeral homes more modest and its vehicles less grand. However, reputable funeral directors act as public servants, and when death strikes people unable to pay the actual funeral costs, a modest sum is charged and the establishment absorbs the remainder. The welfare society in most states pays a low standard fee.

I asked funeral directors about ways to simplify the procedure and cut down on costs. Would it be cheaper not to embalm the body? I found no appreciable savings there. Funeral directors operate a business from a high-cost, 24-hour service establishment and costs reflect this. Cremation expenses are less. Willing the body for medical research bears only the possible expense of transportation and is clearly the least expensive.

Memorial societies exist in most states and have come into being in protest to the elaborate ritual of death and its high cost in America. Generally, their stated purpose is to encourage dignity and simplicity in funeral practices. I investigated such groups in the state in which I reside. These societies usually have a formal contract with one or more funeral directors in an area. Joining a society enables you to finalize arrangements within these low cost contracts. Within this plan, cremation is the most common method and in Detroit the costs approximate $250.00. Burial costs about $400.00. Many of these societies have begun in groups of Unitarian convictions and generally plans call for a quick disposal of the body, apart from the family, followed by a simple memorial service. While much of their literature reflects a simplicity which might appeal to the Christian, upon closer examination there is also a lack of commitment to Christian values and Christian hope.

In the final analysis, a Christian funeral is not determined by cost or efficiency, but by the message it proclaims. Here are the believing ones, made in the image of God, taking death's penalty seriously, but without the sorrow of those who have no hope. Here is the community of those who fear God, caring for the living, mourning the loss of the dead. The Christian way of death is not given to the showmanship of self-indulgence or material values; it is a statement to the world about eternal life.

And in a day when death remains man's unconquerable foe, in the face of our vast scientific accomplishment, the Christian's expression of hope and immortality in the presence of death is a shining light in a dark world.

God

9

God

The God of all comfort . . .
II Corinthians

W hat comes into our minds when we think about God is the most important thing about us.[1] It determines our spiritual future and the way we live in the present.

If I were to ask you to take ten minutes and write down who God is to you, what would you write?

It is not an irrelevant question. The issues of life and death hang on the character of God. The person who comes to a right belief about God is the freest of men. Myriads of temporal problems and perplexities about eternity fall off his back. He no longer carries the weight of responsibility for a world he cannot control. He is content to let God be God.

It is not our ideas *about* God, but *God* who matters. The importance of expressing what we think about God is only to reveal what is rubble in our thinking and what is true. The real God often lies buried in the heap of wrong ideas we've collected about Him. Does it matter if we know the

---

[1]*The Knowledge of the Holy*, A. W. Tozer, (Harper and Row).

real God? Infinitely. We can never know who or what we are until we know something of God. Our ground of existence is linked to Him. The most serious question in life is God Himself. In the religions of the world men seek after God; in Christianity we have God *seeking* men and *revealing* His character to them. We are not groping in the dark; we are living in the light of revelation.

Men often want to reduce God to manageable terms. That is why we hear and say arrogant things like "I can't conceive of a God who. . . ." Or "Why does God put up with . . . ?" Or "I don't think God would. . . ." We think beyond ourselves only with great difficulty in being able to conceptualize God. God is infinitely beyond us. He is incomprehensible and unapproachable. Yet He has revealed Himself in the Scriptures and become infinitely near in Jesus Christ. If the lesser would know the greater, the greater must disclose Himself. Amazingly, the eternal God, the Creator, has done this. He is the Initiator. It is so staggering that some men will not believe it.

The revelation of God strains language. That is why the Bible uses *like* or *the likeness of* — because the revelation must be one man can understand. God has disclosed His character to us in the history of the Old Testament, always promising to intervene in human history with salvation. The story of the New Testament is summed up by John:

> The Word (Jesus Christ) became flesh and dwelt among us, full of grace and truth; we beheld his glory, glory as of the only Son from the Father.
>
> No one has ever seen God; the only Son, who is in the bosom of the Father, he has made him known.
>
> John 1:14, 18

What is the nature of God's character? When we read *God is love* that does not simply mean that He acts lovingly. *God is love* is a fact, not a definition. It is what He is. This is true of all His attributes. God is love. His love knows no bounds. God is constant. He *is* in His essential being whatever attributes He has disclosed to us — and He is in perfect harmony. Nothing in God is more or less, or great or small. He is simply God. He is what He is in Himself. How comforting to turn from our limitations to a God who has none.

This knowledge led Moses to sing

> Lord, thou hast been our dwelling place in all generations. Before the mountains were brought forth, or ever thou hadst formed the earth and the world, from everlasting to everlasting thou art God.   Psalm 90

God is all-wise. His wisdom sees everything in focus. He is able to work toward an eternal plan with precision, not deterred by the waywardness of men. Nothing takes Him by surprise; He never wonders what He will do. He is all-knowing. No one can inform Him about us or tattle any secret to Him. He knows us completely. He knows our frailty, our potential, our affliction.

God is good. The goodness and love of God mean that He has charged Himself with full responsibility for our lives and is willing to take over management if we turn to Him. God, in *being* love and goodness, has planned for our highest good. The wisdom of God plans it; the power of God achieves it, and He is kind.

> For the mountains may depart, and the hills be removed; but my steadfast love shall not depart from you and my covenant of peace shall not be removed, says the Lord who has compassion on thee.   Isaiah 54

God is faithful; He is constant. He is the same yesterday, today and forever. We don't have to wonder how He will react today, what mood He will be in tomorrow morning.

He is constant in all His attributes — constant in love, constant in His availability, constant in His justice, goodness, wisdom and power — because these are facets of the essential nature of God. God does not change in His concern for men; He never tires or loses His enthusiasm for what He has begun. *I am the Lord; I change not!*[2]
Read Isaiah 40 and absorb some of the wonder of His being.

> Have you not known? Have you not heard?
> The Lord is the everlasting God,
>   the Creator of the ends of the earth.
> He does not faint or grow weary,
>   his understanding is unsearchable.

This trustworthiness of God's behavior in His world has made scientific truth possible. Scientific "laws" are simply observations of God's faithfulness.

God is omnipresent. He is everywhere, always near. That is a great truth to put to work in life. God's presence knows no geographical or spatial limits — up, down, across and beyond. The reality of this truth was impressed simply to me one weekend when we left our little son with friends. He was so glad to see us when we returned and clung so tightly that I began to question the wisdom of ever having left. But then a small voice spoke a great truth, "Know what? God can be every place. He was here with me and He was away with you." God is in the far-flung places of the earth. He is infinitely near. No son or daughter, no husband or wife — no one can go where He is not. Read Psalm 139.

God is holy — holiness beyond our imagination. Holy is the way God is. He does not conform to a standard; He is the standard.[3] He is sovereign. He is perfectly just.

---

[2]Malachi 3:6.
[3]*The Knowledge of the Holy*, A. W. Tozer.

The harmony, the perfection, the splendor, the creativity within the character of God tell us that God is joy. Gladness, mirth, joyfulness beyond measure spring out of the very nature of God. When He spoke in creation the morning stars sang together. He touches a man's life and puts a song of praise in his heart. The Psalmist could sing of "God, my exceeding joy," (Psalm 43:4) and reiterate "In thy presence is fulness of joy" (Psalm 16:11). Joy is a heavenly commodity; it exists in full measure wherever God is. It has even caused men to sing at a graveside. That is why Jesus said He came to earth "that they might have my joy fulfilled in themselves" (John 17:13).

All that God does must be in accord with what God is. He cannot act out of character. He is who He is. Justice is present in mercy; love is present in justice. His will and His love are the same.

We rest in what God is — and find His character vastly comforting. This one is *the God of all comfort.* Faith is confidence in the character of God.

We see this God move into the pages of the New Testament and meet Him in Jesus Christ. We see afresh that all the promises of God are *yes* in Jesus Christ.[4] In a conversation with His disciples, Jesus said, "If you have known me, you have known my Father also. He who has seen me has seen the Father."[5]

Christ moves among men in holiness, in goodness. He is tenderhearted and sympathetic. He listens to men, He comes to them — not because He is indebted to them, but because He is merciful.

> He doth give His joy to all:
> He becomes an infant small,
> He becomes a man of woe,
> He doth feel the sorrow too.

---

[4]II Corinthians 1:20.
[5]John 14:7, 9.

Think not thou canst sigh a sigh,
And thy Maker is not by:
Think not thou canst weep a tear,
And thy Maker is not near.

WILLIAM BLAKE

He is forgiving, considerate, hospitable, kind. We see Him and come to love Him. Fear toward God is turned to faith; love casts out fear. Faith is standing in awe of who God is and not being afraid.

We have only skimmed the surface of the infinite character of God. The Bible tells us much more than this, yet *all* that can be said of His trinity, His self-existence, His self-sufficiency, His eternity is beyond us. What we have seen is enough to know that our experience of Him has only just begun.

I have said before that all our peace in this life and in death hangs on the character of God. He has told us who He is. Our lack of faith reflects not on His character, but on ours. Faith is confidence that what He says is true.

Recently in a group discussion on the eighth chapter of the book of Romans, a young widow shared her own experience with us. In her girlhood she had discovered Romans 8: 28 and the following verses which affirm that nothing is able to separate us from the love of God in Christ Jesus. That chapter became her favorite. Years passed and life was rich and full. When her husband was suddenly killed everything good seemed to end. Her minister came to comfort her and asked if she had any favorite Bible passage she would like him to read with her. She mentioned Romans 8, and listened with new awareness as he read,

> We know that in everything God works for good with those who love him, who are called according to his purpose.

They had been favorite words to her in a superficial sense. It had been easy to say them and to believe them before. Now her life lay in shambles; the beauty was all gone. Could it still be her favorite verse? Could she still say, *I know . . . God works for good?*

She had tested it with time, and we waited to hear her conclusion. The words came out between tears, but what she said was genuine. Yes, it is true, she said, I know that in *everything* God works for good.

She does not understand what happened or why. She simply has turned instead to her knowledge of the goodness of God, to the reliability of His character — to God Himself.

> Darkness to the intellect
> But sunshine to the heart.

I speak to myself. I have not faced death's worst dissolution of my life. Will "the rope" hold in such a day? I feel such human reluctance to give up anyone I love. I feel the fear of life without them. And yet, having said that, I know from every past experience that God is utterly trustworthy, that in the wonder of all that He is He will take the pieces of my life and work for my good. I rest in what God is.

Some years ago I did the exercise I recommended earlier in this chapter. I wrote down my scattered thoughts about the character of God:

> God is Father; He is my Father. As Father He is the Originator, the Source of all that is. As Father He is also Redeemer, my Redeemer, the Safe Place, *El Shaddai,* the God who is enough.

> God is the Great Innovator, bringing to fruition all that is His pleasure. Limitless in knowledge and power, He is the great Lion who devours kings and kingdoms. Yet He is also the One who intervenes so that a widow who trusts

Him has her son restored or finds the cruse of oil does not run dry.

He is the One who first loved so that I might know what love is all about. He is the One who gave the eye, the ear, the mind, and the aesthetic sense that causes me to reach out beyond my human smallness to rejoice in a sunset and comprehend a beautiful piece of music. He is the Source of all wisdom and joy.

I stand in awe of His holiness. I cannot comprehend the vastness of it, the quality of it. How can One so terrible in justice and holiness be at the same time so rich in love and mercy? Yet I experience the reality of His grace, His forgiveness, His love — the safeness of knowing Him. His righteous judgments terrify me; His love overwhelms me. The completeness of His forgiveness breaks my proud self.

As a child I used to picture myself sitting on God's lap, safely tucked in the circle of His loving arms. I knew He was the Judge, that He worked in the world beyond and through the evil He found there and that He knew everything. But He loved *me*. Intellectually I know God is a Spirit, that He has no lap. Emotionally my reactions to Him have not left the safety of childhood. His sovereignty and His Fatherhood have been my delights.

I meet God in Jesus Christ. He is the One who can weep at Lazarus' death and then by His Power, the Power which holds the universe together, bring Lazarus back from the dead. He is the One who never compromises truth because He is Truth. At the same time He is full of grace, because He is Grace.

I cannot think up to Him, least of all beyond Him. So He has come to me, revealing Himself according to my capacity, lovingly at work in the small details of my life, while at the same time ruling as the Sovereign of all creation. God is beyond my description; He is beyond my experience of Him. But this I know, He is my Father.

I add this personal note from my journal to emphasize that knowing the God of all comfort is a personal matter. Facts about God are not enough; it is relationship with God that is infinitely comforting.

Jesus Christ spoke of this relationship in the Sermon on the Mount. In discussing the anxieties so common to men, He said, "Don't be anxious. Your heavenly Father knows. . . ." *Your heavenly Father.* A truth so obvious, so intimate: the Christian name for God is Father. Surely the Fatherhood of God *is* at the core of the universe.

If you have ever seen the care, the grace, the peace and the joy the heavenly Father gives those who trust Him, even when life has been shattered, you will know what I have been saying is true. This *quality life* cannot be denied as forcible evidence that God is beyond both life and death.

Out of the struggle of his soul, George Matheson, the blind poet and scholar, wrote the familiar hymn,

> O Love that wilt not let me go,
> I rest my weary soul in Thee;
> I give Thee back the life I owe,
> That in Thine ocean depths its flow
> May richer, fuller be.

There is no other comfort like that given by *the God of all comfort.*